CHRISTIAN HEROES: THEN & NOW

ADONIRAM JUDSON

Bound for Burma

CHRISTIAN HEROES: THEN & NOW

ADONIRAM JUDSON

Bound for Burma

JANET & GEOFF BENGE

YWAM
PUBLISHING

P.O. BOX 55787   SEATTLE, WA 98155

YWAM Publishing is the publishing ministry of Youth With A Mission (YWAM), an international missionary organization of Christians from many denominations dedicated to presenting Jesus Christ to this generation. To this end, YWAM has focused its efforts in three main areas: (1) training and equipping believers for their part in fulfilling the Great Commission (Matthew 28:19), (2) personal evangelism, and (3) mercy ministry (medical and relief work).

For a free catalog of books and materials, call (425) 771-1153 or (800) 922-2143. Visit us online at www.ywampublishing.com.

Adoniram Judson: Bound for Burma
Copyright © 2000 by YWAM Publishing

Published by YWAM Publishing
a ministry of Youth With A Mission
P.O. Box 55787, Seattle, WA 98155

ISBN 978-1-57658-161-2 (paperback)
ISBN 978-1-57658-565-8 (e-book)

Seventh printing 2017

Printed in the United States of America

CHRISTIAN HEROES: THEN & NOW

*Available in paperback, e-book, and audiobook formats. Unit study
curriculum guides are available for select biographies.*

www.HeroesThenAndNow.com

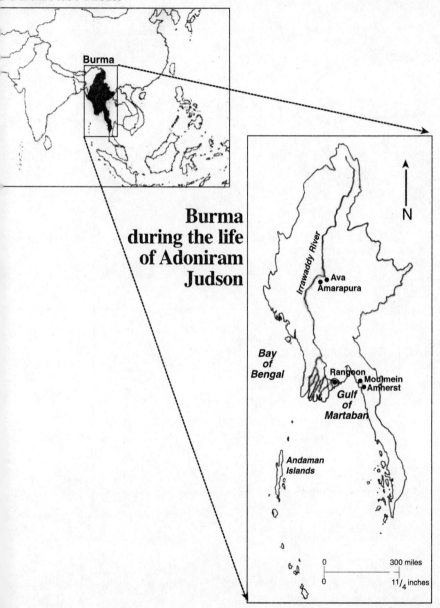

Southeast Asia

Burma

Burma during the life of Adoniram Judson

N

Irrawaddy River

Ava
Amarapura

Bay of Bengal

Rangoon

Moulmein
Amherst

Gulf of Martaban

Andaman Islands

0   300 miles
0   1 1/4 inches

Contents

Something Was Wrong

Twenty-two-year-old Adoniram Judson awoke to the gentle rolling of the *Packet*, the three-masted schooner that was carrying him from Boston across the Atlantic Ocean to London. It was the fifteenth day of the voyage, and after he'd had breakfast with the captain, Adoniram planned to spend the remainder of the day in his cabin reading. He would have much preferred to sit on deck while he read, but it was mid-January 1811, and a raw, biting breeze straight from the Arctic had been whipping around the ship for several days, making it impossible to stay on deck for more than a few minutes at a time, even when the sun was shining brightly.

As he climbed from his bunk, Adoniram wondered whether the only other two passengers

Myanmar = Burma

aboard, both men, would be joining him and the captain for breakfast. The other men spoke only Spanish, and it was amusing trying to work out what they were saying from hand gestures and other forms of body language. Normally, the *Packet* would have had twenty passengers aboard, but the ongoing war between England and France meant that only the most desperate or determined passengers risked crossing the Atlantic Ocean these days, especially aboard a British ship.

WAR! DANGER
?
Determined

As a passenger, Adoniram fit the latter category. He was determined to get to London and meet with the leaders of the London Missionary Society. He had been sent out on behalf of the newly formed Congregational church missionary society, or American Board, as it was called, to ask the London society for money and support so that the fledgling mission could send out the first group of American foreign missionaries. If all went well, Adoniram and the other three missionaries waiting in New England for his return could all be in East Asia by Christmas.

wanted $$ to send 1st American missionary if succ-essful him & buddies could be missionaries

As he splashed some water on his face, Adoniram noticed that something was wrong. Instead of the gentle creaking of the hull of the *Packet*, he heard the sound of feet pounding across the deck above him. He could hear voices, too. It sounded as if everyone was yelling at once. Pulling his pants and jacket on, Adoniram quickly made his way up on deck to investigate.

?
Overthrown by French

Once on deck he saw what all the fuss was. A French ship, its sails billowing in the stiff breeze, was skimming across the water towards them. In response, the crew were darting about the deck hoisting sails and tightening halyards as the captain and first mate barked orders. As he yelled, the captain spun the wheel of the *Packet*, trying to maneuver the ship to take maximum advantage of the wind.

"A privateer," yelled the captain when he spotted Adoniram. "She's armed to the gunwales, and we're trying to outrun her."

Within a few minutes, Adoniram realized that despite the crew's frenzied effort, the French ship was still gaining on them.

Adoniram had heard about French privateers and the way they plundered British ships. He had also heard horror stories of the end some sailors had met at the hands of privateers. Now that it seemed certain that the *Packet* would be overrun by the French ship, he wondered what his end would be. He was an American, and he hoped that that would protect him. But he knew that it probably wouldn't protect his belongings from being looted. That thought spurred him to race to his cabin.

Just as Adoniram finished stuffing his three Bibles—one in English, one in Hebrew, and one in Latin—and his fiancee's last letter to him into a cloth bag, two French sailors burst into the cabin. Adoniram turned, shocked at how fast the French privateers had overtaken and overrun the *Packet*. When he had left the deck, the French ship was at least one hundred yards behind them. Now, apparently, the privateers had boarded the *Packet* and taken complete control.

With gestures, Adoniram was ordered up on deck. He was then herded with the rest of the British crew to the starboard side of the ship and forced to climb down a rope over the side and into a waiting longboat. Within minutes of reaching the French ship, Adoniram was thrown into the hold along with the *Packet*'s crew. The dark and dank hold was overcrowded. There was no food, water, or chamber pots. The only illumination was a dull shaft of sunlight that filtered down through the dusty air of the hold.

humid / moist

Dark thoughts taunted Adoniram Judson as he sat in the overcrowded hold. He would never see New England again. It would be only a matter of time before the French privateers dumped him overboard, as they liked to do with their prisoners. Now he would never see East Asia. All his efforts to become a missionary had been in vain. He had given his all just to drown in the middle of the Atlantic Ocean. Hot tears rolled down Adoniram's cheeks. As a child growing up in Wenham, Massachusetts, this was not how he had imagined his life ending.

Scared for his life

- American, Ship, 4 England
- looking, support missions
- A. + 3 friends, missionaries, E. Asia
- Packet, taken, French, privateers
- Future = Bleak!

Chapter 2

Puzzles

Nine-year-old Adoniram Judson lay down the goose quill he had been writing with and picked up the bottle of sand. He shook the sand gently over the paper, blotting the ink. When the ink was dry, he carefully tipped the sand back into the bottle and folded the paper. He placed the paper in an envelope, sealed the envelope with wax, and quietly slipped out of the house. He smiled with relief as he rounded the big elm tree opposite the church and realized that for once his little sister Abigail had not followed him. Adoniram guessed she was probably playing with their baby sister, Mary.

As he walked along the dusty street, Adoniram felt the envelope in the pocket of his woolen pants.

He was on a secret mission, a mission that he hoped would bring him fame!

When he reached the general store, he walked purposefully up the three wooden steps that led to the door. He stopped at the top of the stairs to make sure no one from his father's congregation other than the postmaster was inside. Thankfully, only a farmer and his two children, whom Adoniram did not recognize, were in the store. Adoniram entered the store and walked to the back where the post office was located. He placed the envelope on the counter. "I would like to mail this to Boston, sir," he said politely.

"Boston, eh? And what would a young man like you be wanting with someone in Boston?" quizzed the postmaster. After reading the address on the envelope, he added with a chuckle, "A newspaper editor, is it? Has something been happening around Wenham that I should know about?" He reached over and tousled Adoniram's curly, chestnut brown hair.

Adoniram felt himself blushing. He had not imagined he would have to explain himself to the postmaster.

Just then the door opened and several men entered the store. "You got any of that apple cider left, Jonah?" one of them asked in a booming voice.

To Adoniram's relief, the postmaster took his attention off him. "Sure have, I'll be right with you," he said to the man, placing the letter on the back counter and smiling at Adoniram. "It's as

[handwritten margin notes: "?y", "sneaky", "must be important"]

good as sent, young man," he said. "Now be sure and give my regards to your father. He preached a mighty fine sermon last Sunday."

[margin note: Father is a preacher]

Adoniram nodded politely and headed out the door into the early fall air. As he walked home, he hoped winter would not arrive too soon. The last two winters, 1795 and 1796, had been particularly harsh in Wenham. Although Adoniram liked to play in the snow, sometimes it had fallen so heavily he hadn't been able to get to Master Dodge's school. More than anything else, Adoniram loved going to school.

[margin note: after Revolution]

"Adoniram, it's dinnertime," he heard his mother call later that day.

Adoniram put down the book he was reading and hurried into the kitchen. It was Wednesday, which meant that his mother had roasted a large leg of beef in the open fireplace in the kitchen. The savory aroma of the cooked meat greeted him as he entered the kitchen. As he sat down at the table, he caught a glimpse of something white in his father's hand. Adoniram froze in terror. It was the letter he had mailed two hours before.

[margin note: words]

"Does this belong to you?" his father boomed, waving the letter in the air.

[margin note: Dad doesn't know the letter]

"Yes, it does," stammered Adoniram.

"What is it about?" asked his father, changing to the flat tone Adoniram had long ago learned meant trouble.

"It's the answer to the weekly 'enigma'—you know, the one that's in the newspaper each week. I solved it and was sending in the answer."

"But those puzzles are for adults, not nine-year-old boys," said his father. "Open it and let me see what kind of fool my oldest son was about to make of himself. It's just as well the postmaster had the good sense not to mail it without my permission."

With trembling hands Adoniram took the envelope from his father and broke the seal. He unfolded the page he had written on so hopefully earlier that afternoon.

"Read it out loud to me. This will be the last time you try to do anything behind my back, young man," growled his father.

Adoniram read aloud the letter he had written to the editor explaining the solution to the enigma of the week. He held his breath when he finished, waiting to hear what his father would say.

"Get me the newspaper," ordered his father.

Shares room w/ brother

Adoniram scurried away to the room he shared with his younger brother, Elnathan, to retrieve the newspaper, glad to be out of his father's presence for a moment. He grabbed the paper from his bed and walked with dread back to the kitchen. "Here it is, sir," he said, handing the newspaper to his father.

Mr. Judson read the puzzle and then compared it to his nine-year-old son's answer. He repeated the process a second and a third time. "Huh," he finally said, laying the paper down and staring at the fire for a few moments.

Mary = baby

Adoniram waited for him to say more, but the only sound in the room was the crackle of the fire and the occasional tiny cough from Mary, tucked in her crib in the corner.

After what seemed like the longest minute of Adoniram's life, his mother finally said in an overly cheerful voice, "Husband, would you be so kind as to carve the meat, and then we'll be ready to eat. I've cooked some fine carrots that Mrs. Grady brought in this morning. Wasn't that kind of her?"

"Hand me the knife," replied Adoniram's father.

After dinner, Adoniram's father read a passage from the Bible, as he always did, and then the three children were dismissed to do their cleanup chores. Adoniram emptied the water that had been heating over the fire into a large wooden bucket and began washing the dishes. Abigail, who had hardly spoken a word the whole meal, dried the dishes and stacked them neatly on the sideboard. Four-year-old Elnathan put the dishes away, except for the breakable china, which Adoniram put back on the shelf above the pantry cupboard.

Not another word was said about the letter, and as Adoniram curled up in bed next to Elnathan that night, he wondered what his punishment would be for sending the letter without his father's permission.

The following morning nothing was said about the letter, and Adoniram was more nervous than ever. Finally, when he arrived home from school, his father called to him, "Adoniram, come here."

Adoniram walked into the living room, where his father was seated in his brown leather wingback chair beside the fire. "I have something for you," his father said.

Adoniram stared in astonishment as his father offered him a book.

"I have bought you a book of puzzles. When you finish it, I will buy you a more difficult one."

Adoniram took the book, unable to think of what to say.

"You are a very smart boy," continued his father. "Your mother and I have known that since you learned to read when you were three. Train your mind, son, and you will be a great man someday."

"Yes, sir. Thank you, sir," stammered Adoniram, hardly able to take in such praise from his father.

"And one more thing. I am going to enroll you in Captain Morton's School of Navigation. How would you like that?" asked his father.

"Yes, sir, very much," replied Adoniram, wanting more than anything to escape to his room where he could be alone to think.

Finally, in his room, Adoniram sat on the bed and thought about the things his father had and hadn't said. He hadn't said anything about how well Adoniram had done answering the enigma in the newspaper, but from his father's reaction, he decided he must have done reasonably well. And what his father said about his being smart was true. Everyone in school knew it. The other students had nicknamed him "Virgil" because of the speed at which he could read and write Greek and Latin, and arithmetic was so easy for him that he had all the answers figured out before his teacher had finished explaining the lesson to the rest of the class. He could name all the thirteen states and their capitals and was able to recite all of George Washington's

inaugural speech by heart. Despite this, his father's
words had surprised him. Did he, Adoniram Judson,
have what it took to be a great man? But then, what
was a "great" man? Was it a preacher like his father?
What about a teacher like Master Dodge? Or a sea
captain like his grandfather? Adoniram did not
know.

True to his word, Mr. Judson enrolled Adoniram
in the navigation school in nearby Salem, the richest
town in New England. Adoniram loved attending
the school, where he learned to use a sextant to
take readings from the sun and stars to chart his
position, as well as how to read marine maps so as
not to run aground. But even more than the school,
he loved being in Salem. When his father came to
visit, they walked together all the way from Derby
Wharf to Crowninshield's Wharf, watching as exotic
cargo from far-off ports in China and Europe was
unloaded. As they watched, brilliantly colored par-
rots from the Malay Islands fluttered their wings in
the gentle breeze or perched on their owners' shoulders. And the smell of unknown spices filled the air.

Three weeks after Adoniram began attending
the new school, disaster struck the Judson family. Six-month-old Mary died. She had been sick
for several weeks and eventually got so weak she
just stopped breathing. All of the Judson children
were saddened by her death, but none more than
Adoniram. He had recently been paying closer
attention to his father's sermons and knew that in
his father's opinion a child, even a tiny baby, had to

make a decision to become a Christian or would be damned to hell. As he looked down at his tiny sister in her white smocked dress lying in a wooden coffin, Adoniram wondered about a God who would be so cruel as to send his innocent sister to hell. Something about it didn't seem right, and although he was far too scared to discuss it with his father, he secretly wanted nothing more to do with the God his father preached about so passionately in church on Sunday mornings.

No sooner had Mary been buried than Mr. Judson became ill. He was so sick that the doctor told him if he did not rest at Saratoga Springs in New York, he too would die. So Adoniram's father spent six weeks recuperating at Saratoga Springs. However, when he finally returned to Wenham he was not much better. Since there was no way he could fulfill all his duties as pastor, on October 22, 1799, he resigned from his position in the church.

As a new century dawned, the Judson family found themselves in a precarious situation. They had moved to Braintree, several miles south of Boston, where Adoniram's father thought he could find work. Indeed, he found a job, but it paid so little that Abigail Judson, Adoniram's mother, found herself eking out the family budget from only a third of the money her husband had been earning in Wenham. Somehow the Judsons managed to scrape together enough money to keep their three children in school. Adoniram continued to outshine his peers academically.

In 1797, there had been great celebrations in Braintree (today called Quincy) as a farmer and lawyer from the town was elected president of the United States. Adoniram and his father often walked past the farm where John Adams had grown up. As they did so, the conversation was always the same. If John Adams could make something great of himself, so could Adoniram Judson!

The Judson family struggled on in Braintree for two years until the newly established Third Congregational Church of Plymouth, Massachusetts, offered the Reverend Mr. Judson the pastorate of the church. Adoniram's father felt much better now and eagerly accepted, moving the family to Plymouth.

Fourteen-year-old Adoniram loved his new hometown with its bustling population of thirty-five thousand people. On the undeveloped east side of town, his father bought a plot of land that sloped down to the sea where the family built a wonderful new house. The family had lived in the house only a few months when Adoniram himself became very ill. It was a year before he was up and about again and able to return to school. It was 1803, and Adoniram was determined to catch up on all the schoolwork he had missed during the year he was sick. He threw himself into his studies. In fact, he worked so hard that he not only caught up on the year he had missed but also completed his next year's work. He was pronounced ready to go on to college.

Adoniram's father was a graduate of Yale University, but since New Haven, Connecticut, was a long way from Plymouth, he looked for a college closer to home for his eldest son to attend. Harvard University was only fifty miles to the north, but Adoniram's father was not impressed with the religious education given there. It was too watered down for his liking. Eventually, it was decided that Adoniram should attend Rhode Island College at Providence, fifty miles to the south.

On August 15, 1804, just six days after his sixteenth birthday, Adoniram, accompanied by his father, set off by stagecoach for Providence. He carried with him a spare set of clothes and his books, all stuffed into the same old leather duffel bag his father had used when he went to college. As they stood in the August afternoon heat in Providence, waiting for the wooden gates of Rhode Island College to be swung open, questions swirled through Adoniram's mind. What would it be like to be away from his family? He had scooped the academic prizes in his local school, but could he keep up with the influential young men who normally attended colleges such as this? And what kind of man would he be when, after four years of study, he passed back out through the gates with his degree in hand?

- A, very smart
- 6mo Mary died → A. turned away God
- Father, sick, resigned, pastor
- Moved to Plymouth - Father preaching
- Ready 4 college - RIC 16yrs. old

The World Was an Open Book

Adoniram sat nervously at his desk. The astronomy paper in front of him was the last of his entrance exams. It worried him as he looked around. The other students were still bent studiously over their work, but Adoniram could not find anything to add to his paper, and there was still an hour to go. He hoped he had not forgotten something important, and so he read over his answers one more time. Taking examinations was all he had done since arriving at Rhode Island College. So far he had taken Greek, Latin, mathematics, geography, logic, oratory, and philosophy exams. Astronomy was his last exam, and it would be a week before he knew whether he had passed. He hoped he had; otherwise he would not be admitted to the college and would be sent back home.

Finally, the teacher pulled a watch from his pocket and announced it was time to stop. Adoniram quickly handed in his test paper and went for a long walk to try to forget about all the exams.

A week later the results were posted. Adoniram's heart sank as he read the list of freshman students for each subject. His name was not on any of the lists. Just as a cold sweat was breaking out on his forehead, his new friend, Jacob Eames, strolled over to the notice board. "Congratulations, Adoniram," he said. "You've made quite an impact."

Adoniram turned to Jacob. "What do you mean?" he asked, bewildered.

Jacob laughed. "You mean you don't know? Look at this. You've made it into the sophomore classes. Your grades were so good that they're letting you skip your freshman year. I haven't heard of it being done before."

Adoniram swung around and searched the list of sophomore classes. Sure enough, there was his name listed in the second-year classes. "I can hardly believe it!" he said. At this rate he would finish college in three years and not the usual four.

As time went by, Adoniram found he had no difficulty keeping up with a class of boys a year older than he. In fact, he was soon running neck and neck with his friend John Bailey for the honor of being top student in the class. Although this meant a lot of study for Adoniram, he managed to

fit in fun times with his friends. John Bailey and
Jacob Eames, his two best friends, were both from
wealthy families, and they were invited to some of
the most lavish parties in Providence. Adoniram
was invited to go along with them, and he enjoyed
mixing in such rich and intellectual circles. At one
party he even met the extremely wealthy Nicholas
Brown, who had just given an enormous sum of
money to Rhode Island College—so much, in fact,
that the college had changed its name to Brown
University in honor of him.

Mr. Judson knew little of his son's partying.
All he had was a letter from Dr. Messer, the president of the university. Regarding Adoniram, Dr.
Messer had written to Adoniram's father, "A uni-
form propriety of conduct, as well as an intense
application to study, distinguishes his character.
Your expectations of him, however sanguine, must
certainly be gratified. I most heartily congratulate
you, my dear sir, on that charming prospect which
you have exhibited in this very amiable and promising son...."

Not only did Mr. Judson have no knowledge of
Adoniram's partying, he also had no idea of something he would have considered a hundred times
worse. Adoniram's friend Jacob Eames was a Deist.
Jacob did not believe that the Christian religion was
any more important or true than any other religion
in the world. He believed there was a god, but that
God had little or no interest in the lives of people.
Many well-known people in 1806 were Deists,

time frame

among them the inventor Benjamin Franklin and the great revolutionary writer Thomas Paine.

As Jacob and Adoniram talked about what they believed, Deism began to make a lot of sense to Adoniram, who decided to become a Deist himself, though he decided never to tell his father. That would put an end to his college career right then and there.

Future??

Not only did they talk about religion, Jacob Eames and Adoniram also spent many hours discussing their futures. What would they be? Where would they go? The world was an open book for a young man with a degree. They imagined themselves as senators, judges, even the president of the United States.

The three years at Brown University passed quickly and happily for Adoniram. During his last year, Adoniram set himself the goal of becoming valedictorian, first in his graduating class. His father heartily encouraged him in this pursuit. They

No money = no school

were both upset, though, when money ran low and Adoniram had to drop out of college for six weeks to teach in Plymouth to earn the money needed to finish out the year at Brown. Still, Adoniram was a determined young man, and once back at college, he soon caught up on his missed courses. At the end of his senior year, he sent the shortest letter he had ever written home to his father. It read: "Dear

Smart

Father, I have got it. Your affectionate son, A.J." Of course, the "it" was the honor of being valedictorian. The entire Judson family glowed with pride as commencement was held on September 2, 1807.

Having graduated, Adoniram was expected to do something important, but what? He had no particular interests, so to fill in time while he planned his future, nineteen-year-old Adoniram went home and opened a small school, which he named the Plymouth Independent Academy. Dismayed by the poor quality of the textbooks available to his students, he wrote two of his own: *Elements of English Grammar* and *The Young Lady's Arithmetic*. Both books were well written, and with the backing of the president of Brown University, both were published that year.

All of this should have made Adoniram proud, but it did not. He was bored. He was living with his family again, and his father expected him to take part in family Bible reading and prayer. Adoniram could hardly stand it as his father droned on from the Bible after each meal. He was a Deist and didn't have time for such trivial things as Bible reading, though he dared not tell his father that.

Finally one day, when Adoniram was twenty years old, he decided he'd had enough of being a schoolteacher. He wanted to experience some of the excitement he and Jacob Eames had talked about so often in college. And when he asked himself where he would find such excitement, there was only one answer: New York City!

"New York?" his mother gasped, the color draining from her face. "You can't be serious, Adoniram! Whatever would make you want to go there?"

"I forbid it!" snapped his father. "New York is a den of iniquity. No son of mine is going to New York."

Adoniram stood beside the fire, staring at the kitchen wall. This was exactly the reaction he had expected. He knew his parents wouldn't be able to accept his closing the school and moving away.

His mother sat down in a high-backed chair and in a gentle voice tried to coax her son not to follow through with his plans. "Adoniram, what's wrong with being a schoolteacher? You have a good reputation with the parents of your students. More boys are ready to enroll next year. Within five years you could be running the largest academy in Plymouth."

"Being a schoolteacher isn't for me, Mother." Adoniram replied gently. "I liked it well enough for a year, but it isn't something I would want to make my career."

"Well, if being a schoolteacher isn't to your liking, enter the ministry, son," interjected his father. "It was good enough for me, and it should be good enough for you. What about it? Are you man enough to step into your father's shoes?"

Adoniram felt his blood pressure rising. A pastor? Didn't his parents understand him at all? In a flash of rage he opened his mouth, and the words flowed out. "I would rather go to hell than be a pastor. But if you must know, I don't believe in hell or heaven, or your God, or any of your petty little doctrines. I am a Deist, and I have been so for three years."

The kitchen was completely silent. Adoniram's father's eyes bulged, his mother's mouth gaped. Elnathan unwittingly walked into the room, took one look at his parents' faces, and fled. A full minute ticked by. Finally, just as Adoniram thought he would have to do something to break the awful silence, his father spoke. It was as though a dam had burst within him. He strode over to his son, looked him squarely in the eyes, and asked in a growl, "Who did this to you? Was it one of your professors at Brown? Give me his name, and I'll see he's strung up by his thumbs!"

Mr. Judson ranted on for several minutes and then all at once calmed down. "Abigail," he said, turning to his wife, "please leave the room. I have something I wish to discuss with Adoniram."

Adoniram's mother quickly stood and left, mopping away the tears that streamed down her cheeks. All afternoon and into the evening Mr. Judson argued with his son. Point by point he went through the beliefs of the Deists, trying to poke holes in their arguments. But after several hours, he shrugged his shoulders. "For every point I raise, you raise a better one," he finally told Adoniram. "Your teachers at Brown University have taught you well. You argue with logic and clarity. But I will tell you one thing. No matter how good your arguments are, you are wrong. We will not discuss this again, but I pray one day you will find out the truth for yourself." With that he lit his pipe and stared blankly at the fire.

Adoniram got up and left the room. He should have felt very smug at that moment. He had flexed his intellectual muscles against his father and had won hands down, but his mother made feeling smug impossible. While his father had relied on logical thinking to try to win back Adoniram, Mrs. Judson cried and pleaded with her son. Every moment Adoniram was at home she followed him around, praying that God would help him to see the truth.

Adoniram could take the pressure of his mother's tears for only so long. After six days of her following him around, he packed a few belongings into a saddlebag, mounted a horse, and in mid-August 1808 headed west into country he had never seen before.

As he rode into the countryside, Adoniram was fascinated with the new landscape. He loved the rolling hills sparsely dotted with farms. In Springfield he stopped to eat bread by the Connecticut River. As the day progressed, a plan developed in his mind. He would ride to Sheffield and spend the night with his Uncle Ephraim. He would leave his horse there and walk to Albany, New York. Waiting at Albany was a strange new invention Adoniram had read about: the _Clermont_, Robert Fulton's steamboat. It was said to be the first successful steamboat in the world. It went all the way from Albany down the Hudson River to New York City. Adoniram even gave some thought as he rode as to what he might do once he got to

New York. He and Jacob Eames had often talked about becoming famous American playwrights, and Adoniram decided this would be his golden opportunity. New York was known for its theater district and great variety of entertainment.

When Adoniram finally stepped ashore onto Manhattan Island at the mouth of the Hudson River, one hundred sixty miles downriver from Albany, he already had the ideas for several plays running through his mind. He felt sure that all he needed was to hook up with a suitable group of ambitious young men like himself and he would go far in the new life he had chosen for himself.

A week later, Adoniram was not so sure about things. He had not met any young men he thought creative or witty and in desperation had joined a group of roving players. These men were uneducated and unscrupulous. Since none of them earned a steady income, their main entertainment was finding new ways to cheat others. One of their favorite scams was to arrange lodging at one of the hundreds of flea-infested flophouses around the dock area and sneak out before dawn without paying their bill. Adoniram felt guilty doing this, but what else could he do? He had no money of his own to rent a decent room, and his dreams of earning money as a playwright were dissolving fast. Many people told him the New York theaters were having their worst year ever financially, and unless he could juggle or do acrobatics, he had little hope of finding a job in one of them.

Bad conditions

Adoniram persevered for a month—a month of sleeping in a succession of lumpy beds or on hard parlor floors, a month of eating oatmeal three times a day, and a month of hearing over and over that there were no openings in the theater for a twenty-year-old with no experience in playwriting or directing. By the middle of September, he'd had enough. His dream of taking New York by storm, of being the Shakespeare of the United States, was in tatters. Adoniram wanted nothing more than to escape the noise, overcrowding, and filth of New York and to seek his fortune elsewhere. As he packed his few belongings into a bag, he had just one thing on his mind: He would collect his horse from his uncle in Sheffield and head farther west. There, he was convinced, lay his path of opportunity.

- Becomes Deist
- Friends - Jacob Eames
- Post-grad, home, opens school
- Bored, NYC, play
- Parents, appalled
- Deism revealed
- NYC - struggles
- Broke, Filthy, miserable
- Plan - Farther West

Chapter 4

Questions

Since this time Adoniram did not have enough ~~Broke~~
money for the luxury of a steamboat ride, he set
out on the long walk up the Hudson River valley
to his uncle's home, where he planned to collect his
horse. He slept in haystacks and worked for farm-
ers in exchange for meals. As he made his way, he
wondered what had gone wrong. He had set out
from Plymouth with such high hopes, but they had
all come to nothing. He wondered also what had
become of Jacob Eames. Together they had made so
many plans, and now Adoniram was without any
plan. He had tried everything he thought would
make him happy, but nothing had. He was sure
that somehow things had worked out better for
Jacob Eames. Jacob was probably working for some

important law firm by now, well on his way to becoming a famous attorney or even a senator.

Finally, after several days of walking, Adoniram arrived back in Sheffield. His horse was there, but not his uncle. Instead he was met at the parsonage door by a man just a few years older than he. The young man introduced himself as a newly ordained minister who had been sent to fill in for his uncle for two weeks while he was away on business. He invited Adoniram to spend the night, and since the sun was already setting over the Catskill Mountains, Adoniram accepted the invitation.

setting

Later that evening after dinner, the conversation turned to religion. Adoniram was used to arguing about religion with his friends at college and with his father, but this young pastor was different. While Adoniram could hold his own in the conversation, deep down he had to admit the young man had something he longed for. The young pastor seemed to have a direction for his life and peace of mind. Later that night, as he lay on a soft, flealess mattress for the first time in weeks, Adoniram wondered whether he could accept the kind of religion the young pastor had. After thinking about if for some time, he finally rolled over, pulled the blanket tight around himself, and decided he couldn't.

The following day, Adoniram left a note thanking his uncle for keeping his horse, said farewell to the young pastor, and set off westward. Fall had come early that year, and he was fascinated with the waves of red and gold leaves that bobbed in the wind for as far as he could see. He rode on all day, and at nightfall he came to a small village. Adoniram tied up his horse at the local inn and went in to rent the cheapest room available for the night.

setting - Bar ↑, inn

Inside Adoniram found a man with enormous hands pouring ale for customers who were seated around the bar and at tables dotted throughout the smoke-filled room. Adoniram guessed the man was the innkeeper and walked over to him. "Good evening, sir," he began. "I was wondering if you have a room for a weary traveler."

The man finished pouring a <u>tankard</u> of ale before turning to face Adoniram. "A weary traveler? And where might you be coming from?" he asked.

"Sheffield," replied Adoniram.

The innkeeper raised his eyebrows. "That's quite a ride you've had, but unfortunately the inn is full."

"Full?" repeated Adoniram, before breaking into a smile as he thought about all the rat holes in which he had slept in New York City. "I can assure you, sir, I'm not picky. Isn't there a bed somewhere I could sleep in, or even a mat by a fire? I don't know these parts, and I'm reluctant to ride on after dark."

"And so you should be," replied the innkeeper. "There's been some bad things happening after dark in these parts." He squinted at Adoniram. "I'll tell you what. I have a room, partitioned off with a sheet. One half is already occupied, has been all week, by a dying man. He needs to be attended to through the night, and he groans in pain. If you can stand the noise, the other half of the room is available. It even has a bed."

Adoniram grinned. "Thank you. I've ridden hard today, and I can assure you nothing will keep me awake tonight!"

But he was wrong. Once he had fed and watered his horse and had eaten dinner, Adoniram climbed the stairs to his half of the room. He lay down on the bed and stared up at the ceiling crossbeams, unable to fall sleep. Through the sheet that partitioned the room he could hear the footsteps of people coming and going and the loud groans of a man and the whispers of a woman.

In the distance a bell rang out midnight, and then one o'clock, and still Adoniram had not managed to fall asleep. When the bell struck three o'clock, he found himself thinking about the man in the other half of the room. Who was he? Had he done everything he wanted to in his life? Did he know he was dying, and did he fear death? Then he began asking himself the same questions. In the dark, miles from home, and without any plan for his future, Adoniram's Deist beliefs, which had seemed so fine in college, were empty and joyless. He thought about the young pastor at his uncle's house, and he envied the man's sense of purpose in life.

After a while he switched his thoughts back to the dying man. Where would he be buried? Did he believe in life after death, or did he think his soul would rot right along with his body? After letting his mind wander down these paths for nearly an hour, Adoniram came to his senses. What was he thinking? He was an intelligent young man, college valedictorian, and winner of debates and arguments. He could almost hear Jacob Eames laughing at him for indulging in such pointless thinking.

Finally, at about four o'clock, there was silence on the other side of the sheet, and Adoniram finally drifted off to sleep. As he slept he dreamt of skeletons dancing on graves and ghosts laughing at him. He was glad when the sun rose and it was time to get up. He collected his things and prepared himself for the next leg of his journey westward.

"Is it too late for breakfast?" he asked the innkeeper at the bottom of the stairs, noticing the room was almost empty.

"No. I still have some oatmeal in a pot over the fire. That should stick to your ribs for a while," replied the innkeeper, picking up a wooden bowl from the table and walking over to the fire. "So, how did you sleep? I hope the noise didn't disturb you too much."

"No," lied Adoniram. "And how is the man in the next room?"

"Dead," replied the innkeeper, ladling out a big helping of oatmeal. "He died at about four this morning."

The word *dead* echoed around Adoniram's head. Being the son of a pastor, Adoniram was used to hearing about deaths and funerals. But there was something about this death that unnerved him

"I'm sorry to hear he died," he said. "Who was he, anyway?"

The innkeeper plopped down the bowl of oatmeal in front of Adoniram. "A smart young man by all accounts. They said he had been to college in Providence. Brown University, I think it was."

Adoniram felt the goosebumps rising on the back of his neck. "Do you know his name?" he asked soberly.

Eames = Dead

"Of course," replied the innkeeper. "I've had to send for his family. His name was Eames, Jacob Eames."

Adoniram let out a loud gasp. Jacob Eames was dead! It was almost too unbelievable to grasp. His closest friend from college had died not more than ten feet away from him, and he had not known. Every groan, every rasped breath he had heard in the night was Jacob's. The questions he had asked himself in the night all had answers now. Jacob Eames did not believe in life after death. He did not believe his soul would live on. He was gone forever, and well before he had accomplished the things he'd set out so determinedly to accomplish.

"Are you all right?" asked the innkeeper. "Surely it wasn't someone you knew?"

Adoniram nodded, unable to speak. In fact, he said very little for the next several hours. He just sat by the fire staring into the flames, the bowl of oatmeal now stone cold on the table in front of him. People came and went. Jacob Eames's body was carried out in a pine coffin, but Adoniram did not move. It was well into the afternoon before he had recovered enough from the shock of Jacob's death to saddle up his horse and ride on.

Adoniram had ridden about an hour westward when he could stand it no more. Repeated over and over in the clop of his horse's hooves Adoniram could hear the words "He's dead. He's lost." When he came to a fork in the road, instead of turning right, Adoniram turned his horse completely around and headed back the way he had come. He was going home to Plymouth to get some answers.

When he finally arrived home on September 22, 1808, his parents were surprised to see him. His mother assumed he had come home to reopen the academy, and she bustled around making plans for him. However, Adoniram made it clear to her he did not want to become a schoolteacher again. He did not want to settle back into the life he had left. Thoughts of Jacob Eames's death haunted him, and he needed to decide whether or not he could accept the faith his father had taught him. In his heart, Adoniram felt pulled towards Christianity, which provided so many answers to the questions about having peace and purpose in life. But he had a well-trained mind that would not yield to things that didn't seem logical. There were just too many unanswered questions for him to throw his lot in with his parents' religion.

During his first week at home, Adoniram explained what he was feeling to his parents, but they had no idea how to help him. During his second week at home, two important visitors came to stay with the Judsons. Dr. Stuart and Dr. Griffin were well-respected pastors who had graduated from Yale University. They had come to discuss the final plans for opening a theological seminary in Andover, Massachusetts, where they had both been invited to teach. Mr. Judson had long been interested in the project and supported it in any way he could.

Adoniram plied the two men with questions, but every answer they gave led to another question, and before they could answer all the questions it was time for the guests to leave. However, they had sensed Adoniram's sincerity and made him a strange offer. They invited him to enroll in the new Andover Theological Seminary, not as a regular student going on to become a pastor, but as a non-Christian who wanted to study more about Christianity. Adoniram thanked them for the offer and then turned it down. Instead he went to Boston, where he got a job as an assistant teacher. He was happy enough doing this, except for one thing: the memory of Jacob Eames's death. The questions about it would not go away, and Adoniram knew he would not be happy until he found the answers he sought. As he thought about it, there was only one place where he would find those answers: the new theological seminary in Andover.

On October 12, 1808, Adoniram Judson entered the seminary at Andover. It was not at all like he'd expected. To begin with, Andover was the most remote town he'd ever lived in. Being there was like going back a hundred years. The mail was delivered only three times a week, and there were no newspapers delivered to the town at all. The religion of the pilgrims was still practiced and enforced by law. It was illegal to travel anywhere but church from sundown on Saturday until sundown on Sunday, and all work, including cooking and hobbies, was forbidden during this time. Also, Christian sermons and the Bible were the only things allowed to be read on Sundays. Anyone caught disobeying these laws was thrown into prison.

Life inside the seminary was also like going back in time. The students chopped their own firewood to heat their rooms, drew their own water from the well, and took turns helping the cook, Mrs. Silence Smith. Adoniram smiled at her name, wondering whether she had been a very quiet baby or whether her parents had given her the name in hope she would not grow up to be as loud as her brothers and sisters. The seminary had its own cows, which the students took turns milking. It had hay fields and gardens where the students also did chores. All this work meant that the cost for renting a room was low. Adoniram paid only four dollars a year for his dormitory room. On top of this, the professors gave their teaching time free of charge.

With little else to distract him, Adoniram threw himself into study, hoping to find answers to his questions. He studied the Bible in its original languages, Hebrew and Greek, and spent many hours with Dr. Pearson, who had given up his position as professor of Hebrew and Oriental languages at Harvard University to help start the Andover seminary. Adoniram liked Dr. Pearson a lot, and the two men spent many hours in discussion together.

Christian

Finally, on December 2, 1808, Adoniram quietly came to the conclusion that the Bible was correct and that he should commit his life and future to God. He did this alone, standing under a bare apple tree at the far end of the seminary property. With a cold wind whipping at his face, he prayed a simple prayer and dedicated himself to God. No one was around to witness his commitment, but he didn't care. For the first time in his life that he could recall, he felt free. It was not his father's faith in God he was relying on now, it was his own. Later, as he walked back to his dormitory room, Adoniram wondered what this dedication of his life to God would mean. He had no idea what direction his future would take.

Six months later, in June 1809, Adoniram went home to Plymouth and officially joined his father's Congregational church. It was a day of great joy for him and the whole Judson family, who were all together in one place with one common faith. Adoniram enjoyed the moment, but he had the strangest feeling he would not always be surrounded by people who loved and appreciated him. He couldn't say why he felt that way; he just did.

When Adoniram returned to Andover for his second year, a new professor had joined the staff.

The professor was Dr. Griffin, the same man who had visited the Judson home and encouraged Adoniram to sign up for Andover in the first place. Adoniram was glad to see him again.

Adoniram worked hard in his classes, and since he was a fast worker, he often found himself with extra time on his hands. He liked to pass this time in the small but growing seminary library, reading all the new books and pamphlets donated by pastors in the area.

One day as he rifled through a stack of books, Adoniram came across a pamphlet he had not seen before. It was entitled *The Star of the East*, and it was written by a Dr. Buchanan who had been chaplain to the British East India Company for many years. Adoniram signed the pamphlet out and took it to his room to read. The type was small, and he had to sit by the window to get enough light to read by. As he read, his heart began to race. Dr. Buchanan told how the people of India were steeped in superstition and practiced idolatrous religions, and how the time was right to share the gospel with them. Something stirred deep inside Adoniram. He knew he was staring at his destiny.

Over the next several weeks, Adoniram could hardly pay attention to his studies. His head was filled with the stories he had been reading. There was the story of William Carey, the English shoemaker who had gone as the first Baptist missionary to India, where he had started a thriving Bible translation, printing, and distribution network. And

there was the story of Robert Morrison, who had
managed to translate the Bible into Chinese right
under the noses of the Chinese authorities, who
would have killed him had they any idea what he
was up to.

But most inspiring of all was the book *An
Account of an Embassy to the Kingdom of Ava*, written
by Michael Symes, a British army officer whom
the governor general of India had sent to Burma
in 1795. While the book had lots of dull facts about
the various successes and failures of Symes's dip-
lomatic efforts, shining through its pages was a
glimpse into a strange and distant land—a land
where the king's word was law and a man could
have his hand cut off if he failed to lower his eyes
when the royal shadow passed his way. It was a
land where the people worshiped Buddha and
believed that they each had many lives and that
what they did in this life determined the form in
which they would return. If they were bad, they
might come back in the next life as a rat or an ant; if
they were good, as a prince or princess.

Adoniram read all he could about Burma and
the Buddhist religion. The more he read, the more
convinced he became that God was calling him to
be a missionary to these people. He would be the
first missionary ever to leave the shores of America
for a foreign land. He didn't know how it would
happen, and he didn't know when, but he did
know it would happen.

Chapter 5

A Most Wonderful Opportunity

It was a cold December day in 1809 when Adoniram Judson threw his carpetbag up to the driver and climbed aboard the stagecoach bound for Plymouth. He was looking forward to spending Christmas with his family. After the Christmas break he would return to Andover seminary to finish his final year of study.

As he sat on the wooden bench seat in the stagecoach, staring out the window at the snowy countryside, Adoniram had one question on his mind: How would he tell his parents and his sister, Abigail, that he planned to be America's first foreign missionary? So far he had told no one, not even his professors at Andover, about his plans. But he felt sure that once his family got used to the

47

idea they would be proud of his decision to go to Burma. He imagined his mother quizzing him on how he had come to the decision to go and Abigail asking if he planned to marry first and take a wife with him. And of course his father would want to discuss the theology of missions with him. By the time the stagecoach pulled to a halt in Plymouth, Adoniram had almost convinced himself that his family would be delighted that he had set his heart on becoming a missionary.

For the first three days at home, Adoniram did not mention his secret, and for one simple reason. He began to get the feeling that his family had a secret of their own and were waiting to tell him. Sometimes he would catch his sister and mother whispering together, and when he came close, they would smile at each other and go about their chores. Or his father would make some comment about what a "bright and prosperous future" Adoniram had in front of him.

Finally, on his fourth night at home, Adoniram could not stand the whispering and hints anymore. After dinner, as the family sat around the fire, he stood up and asked in his most matter-of-fact voice, "Father, do you have some plans for my future that you wish to discuss with me, because I have some of my own that I wish to inform you of."

His mother put down her knitting and nodded at Abigail. His father smiled broadly. "Indeed I do, son," he said, "and I'm sure you will be as excited as I am when you hear what has been proposed. Dr. Griffin, your professor at Andover, came to see me two weeks ago. He has been watching your progress since you became a Christian, and he is very impressed with you. So impressed, in fact..." Mr. Judson drew a long puff on his pipe before continuing, "...that when he takes up his new position as pastor of Park Street Church in Boston, he would like you to be his assistant. After you graduate, of course."

Abigail rushed over to her older brother and clasped his hands, her eyes shining. "Isn't it wonderful news. My brother at Park Street, the biggest church in Boston."

Then Mrs. Judson chimed in. "Dr. Griffin thinks it's only the beginning. He says in ten years you will be one of the most prominent pastors in all of New England."

Adoniram heard his father's voice again. "This is a most wonderful opportunity, and we should be very grateful to Dr. Griffin for offering...."

His father's voice faded from hearing as Adoniram struggled to take in the excitement around him. How could he tell them his secret now? He felt sick to his stomach. His parents and sister continued talking over each other, expounding on all the advantages of his new position. After several minutes, though, Adoniram knew he had to say something.

Abigail was still gushing about all the possibilities of the new position. "Just think of it, Adoniram. You will be so close in Boston that sometimes Mother and I will be able to come and hear you preach."

Adoniram held up his hand. "No, Abigail," he said wearily. "I will never live in Boston. I have a lot farther to go than that."

The chatter in the room stopped immediately. All eyes were fixed on Adoniram.

"What do you mean?" demanded his father. "This is the opportunity of a lifetime. Surely you don't mean to turn it down? You could not possibly have been offered a better position."

Adoniram looked from one shocked face to the other. "I'm afraid I cannot take up the offer," he said. "God has called me to Burma to be a missionary."

His mother let out a long gasp, and Abigail sat down beside her with a plunk.

"A missionary?" spluttered his father, looking as though Adoniram had punched him in the stomach. "A missionary to Burma?"

"Oh, Adoniram, you can't," wailed Abigail. "You mustn't." With that she threw her head into her mother's lap and began to sob.

Adoniram looked at his mother. Big round tears were spilling over the edges of her eyes and sliding down her cheeks. His father sat silently puffing on his pipe, a glazed look in his eyes.

The rest of Adoniram's vacation was a nightmare. His father barely spoke, Abigail constantly clung to him, and Mrs. Judson seemed to believe that tears would change her son's mind. They did not, and Adoniram went back to Andover more determined than ever to pursue his dream of becoming America's first foreign missionary.

Adoniram expected that when he got back to the seminary he would be laughed at for throwing away such a good opportunity and hauled into Dr. Griffin's office and asked why he had turned down

the chance of a lifetime. But none of that happened.
Adoniram had been so caught up in his desire to be
a missionary that he hadn't noticed several other
men whose thoughts were also turning towards
foreign missions.

After telling his family of his plans to be a missionary, Adoniram felt free to go ahead and tell
his fellow students. Within a week, everyone at
Andover knew of his far-fetched plans. Many students laughed at him, and others told him to leave
missionary work to the British. After all, they had
missionary societies, while America was still struggling to become a strong nation in her own right. A
student with a different view came to see Adoniram
privately. His name was Samuel Mills, and before
coming to the seminary at Andover, he had been
a student at Williams College. A small group of
students there had pledged themselves to missions
in a secret society they called the Brethren. Once
at Andover, Samuel Mills had managed to interest three other students—Samuel Newell, Samuel
Nott, and James Richards—in becoming members
of the Brethren. Now that Adoniram had stirred
up interest in missions, the students had decided
to invite him to join the group. Their aim, Samuel
Mills told him, was to help each other stay focused
on missions, to pray for opportunities to go as missionaries, and to be ready at all times in case such
an opportunity presented itself.

Adoniram was astonished to hear about such
a group and joined immediately. However, there
was one difference between him and the other four

members. The constitution of the Brethren stated
that each member "shall hold himself in readiness
to go on a mission when and where duty may call."
Adoniram was not content to "hold himself in readiness"; he wanted to go looking for his call.

*Edward
Warren
Luther
Rice*

    By spring 1810, two more students, Edward
Warren and Luther Rice, were invited to join the
Brethren. That brought the total number of the
group to seven. Together they felt the time was
right to stop being a secret group and start sharing
their goals with others. Surprisingly, one man who
was very supportive of them was Dr. Griffin, who

CC

realized that Adoniram had his heart set on becoming a missionary rather than an assistant pastor. Dr.
Griffin did all he could to help.
    Everywhere they went, the members of the
Brethren talked to people about missions. They
preached about it, wrote letters to newspapers
about it, and penned articles for religious magazines. Adoniram wrote a piece he called "Concern

AA

for the Salvation of the Heathen," which was published in two magazines. Interest and enthusiasm reached a peak in early summer 1810. Dr.
Griffin and many other prominent pastors urged

l

the young men in the group to ask the elders of the
Congregational church to begin a missions organization, with the aim of sending some or all of them
out as missionaries.
    Thursday, June 28, 1810, was a date forever
etched in Adoniram's memory. It was the day he
stood before the leaders of the Congregational
church in a simple parish meetinghouse opposite

Kimball Tavern in Bradford, Massachusetts. The one-room meetinghouse was packed with twenty-eight pastors from around the state and about one hundred fifty local people—more people than could be seated at one time. People stood along the walls and in the doorway. The atmosphere was electric as the young man with the long nose and brown curly hair stood to address the leaders of the church. Adoniram Judson straightened the paper he was holding and looked around the room. Every eye was on him, and not a sound was to be heard.

[handwritten margin note: Congregational church - crowded]

Adoniram swallowed hard and then began to read the words written on the page. "The undersigned members of the divinity college respectfully request the attention of their Reverend Fathers. They beg leave to state that their minds have long been impressed with the duty and importance of personally attempting a mission to the heathen...."

A gasp went up from the crowd, but with his voice firm, even though he was trembling inside, Adoniram continued. The petition asked the Congregational general assembly to set up a missionary organization for "their advice, direction, and prayers." Adoniram concluded by reading the names of the four men who had signed the letter, Adoniram Judson Jr., Samuel Nott Jr., Samuel J. Mills, and Samuel Newell.

[handwritten margin note: 4 signatures]

Reading the petition took less than three minutes, but it was the longest three minutes of Adoniram's life. When he sat down, the moderator, Dr. Culter, called the men who had signed the petition one by one to the front to answer questions. As

Adoniram sat listening to their answers, he knew his future and the future of his friends were being decided as they spoke.

When the young men had finished answering all the questions, the meeting was adjourned. Dr. Culter promised that the general assembly would have a formal reply for them the following morning.

The members of the Brethren walked the ten miles from Andover to Bradford early the next morning. One minute they were exuberant about the possibility of being missionaries, and the next minute they doubted that anyone had taken them and their petition seriously.

At nine thirty, the meeting of the general assembly began, and the members of the committee who had discussed the petition late into the night came forward. Adoniram sat completely still, listening to every word Mr. Hale, secretary of the committee, said. "We the committee," Mr. Hale began slowly, "have seriously considered the petition of the young men from Andover Theological Seminary, and we recommend that their purpose be approved and that a foreign missionary board be organized to support these young men and those who may be called to follow them."

The crowd cheered, and Adoniram felt his back being patted and his hand being shaken. Slowly the reality of what Mr. Hale had said sunk in. The way was being paved for him to go to Burma as a missionary.

After all the congratulating was over, Adoniram made his way down the road to Deacon John

Hasseltine's lavish home, where he and a number of the other pastors had been invited for lunch. About twenty men sat down to eat. Adoniram had heard of the deacon's fine hospitality, and he was not disappointed. A dazzling array of pies and cakes was spread on the side table. A young woman about twenty years of age walked purposefully out of the kitchen and began to serve the men.

[margin note: setting - Hasseltine's home]

"Thank you, Ann," said the pastor sitting next to Adoniram, "I can always count on you to know what I want!"

The young woman laughed, and Adoniram turned to look at her. She was about five feet five inches tall, with jet black curly hair, flawless olive skin, and the deepest blue eyes he had ever seen.

[margin note: !! Beautiful Lady :-)]

"So what do you think of the name 'American Board of Commissioners for Foreign Missions'?" The Reverend Mr. Allen asked Adoniram.

Adoniram stared back at him blankly, unable to think of an answer. For the first time in his life he had nothing whatsoever to say!

Throughout the meal Adoniram could not take his eyes off Ann, whom he learned was the youngest of Deacon Hasseltine's five children. As he strolled back to the meetinghouse for the afternoon session, Adoniram was sure of one thing: He was in love.

[handwritten notes at bottom:]
- Wanted to be a missionary in Burma
- Parents X want Ad. to be a miss. → past.
- Friends: Samuel Nott, Samuel Mills, Samuel Newell
- missions trip approved
- Love w/ Ann

Chapter 6

Privateers

A doniram could hardly wait to go back to Bradford again. He used any excuse he could think of to visit the Hasseltine home. And after each visit he was more convinced than ever that he had found the woman he wanted to spend the rest of his life with.

[margin note: mg'd Ann]

After a month of visiting, he knew it was time to write a formal letter to Ann (who was also called <u>Nancy</u> by many of her friends), telling her he had serious intentions towards her. He wrote asking if she was willing to "formally commence an acquaintanceship," which was the proper way to ask a young woman to consider marriage. It was also proper for a young woman not to answer such a letter too quickly, because to do so would make

[margin note: CC wrote letter to Ann]

[margin note: setting]

her look overly eager. So Ann made Adoniram wait an agonizing week before she replied. And in her letter she gave no answer to his request; she just said her parents would have to consent to the relationship before she would even consider the idea.

Adoniram knew he had another letter to write, and it would be the hardest piece of writing he had ever attempted. He wondered how he was going to tell Ann's parents that he would like to marry their beautiful, talented daughter and drag her off to the Far East, where they would probably both die. He tried wording the letter one way and then another. The candle burned low, and his eyes ached with strain before he finally settled on the wording for such an important letter. It read:

I have now to ask, whether you can consent to part with your daughter early next spring, to see her no more in this world; whether you can consent to her departure, and her subjection to the hardships and sufferings of a missionary life; whether you can consent to her exposure to the dangers of the ocean; to the fatal influence of the southern climate of [Burma]; to every kind of want and distress; to degradation, insult, persecution, and perhaps a violent death. Can you consent to all this, for the sake of Him who left His heavenly home, and died for

[handwritten margin notes: "!!" "Parents have to agree to marriage" "11" "will they follow through" "12." "Degradation"]

her and for you; for the sake of perishing,
immortal souls; for the sake of Zion, and
the glory of God?

As he sealed it, Adoniram knew he had written
a bleak letter. He thought of his own parents. How
would they react if someone wrote to them asking
for Abigail's hand in marriage and included in the
letter a list of hardships she could expect to endure?
Still, as blunt as the letter was, he knew it had to be
that way. If Ann Hasseltine was to become his wife,
she would face many hardships, and he did not
want her family to let her go begrudgingly or without thinking of the cost to themselves.

A week later, Adoniram received a reply.
Deacon Hasseltine wrote to tell him that although
he and his wife were not in favor of their youngest daughter going on such a perilous journey,
especially since they may well never see her again,
neither of them would forbid her from going. The
decision as to whether she became Mrs. Judson was
hers alone to make. Whatever she decided, her parents would stand by her decision.

Adoniram continued to pay visits to the
Hasseltine home. The more he learned about Ann,
the less likely he thought it was that she would
give up everything for him. The Hasseltine home
was the center of social activity for miles around, so
much so that Deacon Hasseltine had built an entire
wing onto his house to be used as a dance hall by
the young people of the district.

Ann had been the first person in her family to become a Christian. She was fifteen at the time, and her parents and brother and sisters quickly followed her example. Despite the family's conversion, the lively social events continued at their home, with Ann at the center of them all. Adoniram groaned when he discovered how many young men in the district had their eyes on Ann. Many of them came from rich homes and could give her the kind of life she had grown up with. What were a dangerous sea voyage and unknown hardships in Burma compared to that?

On September 24, 1810, Adoniram Judson graduated from Andover Theological Seminary, though he continued to live in his dormitory room after graduation. Most of the other students were off to be junior or assistant pastors in churches around New England, but Adoniram had nowhere else to go. He was waiting for the American Board, as the Congregational church's new mission organization was called, to tell him what he should do next. He could have waited back home in Plymouth, but there was the matter of Ann. Over the next several weeks, the two of them rode together around the New England countryside, taking in all the beauty of early fall as the leaves began to change color. As they rode, they discussed their views on the Bible, on families, and on missions. Finally, in mid-October, Ann announced she had made up her mind. She would marry Adoniram and go wherever God led them. Adoniram could hardly contain his excitement.

The couple decided they would get married just before they left America, but no one could say for sure when that would be. The American Board had formed a subcommittee called the Prudential Committee, whose job it was to work out how to financially support the missionaries it sent out. This proved a difficult task, and in the end it was decided that the American Board would just have to humble itself before the London Missionary Society and ask if they would provide the money needed to help send and support the missionaries. Of course, this was a blow to almost everyone concerned. Memories of the American Revolutionary War were still fresh in the minds of most people. The last thing any American wanted to do was ask the British for help. Still, they could see no way around the situation, and so on Christmas Day 1810, the would-be missionaries, Samuel Newell, Samuel Nott, Gordon Hall, and Adoniram Judson met with the American Board.

All four young men were formally accepted as missionaries, and Adoniram was chosen to go to London to put their request before the London Missionary Society. Passage was booked to London for him aboard the *Packet*, a three-masted schooner scheduled to sail from Boston on New Year's Day 1811.

Bad weather delayed the *Packet*'s departure, and the ship finally sailed out of Boston Harbor on January 11. Once out of sight of land, Adoniram spent most of his time reading. There was little else to do on the small ship, and there were only two other passengers, both of whom spoke only Spanish. Normally the ship would have carried about twenty passengers, but war was raging between England and France, and it was rumored that the United States might soon go to war against both countries. Only desperate or determined passengers risked sailing across the Atlantic at this time, and Adoniram was soon to find out just how much of a risk it was.

On the fifteenth morning of the voyage, Adoniram awoke to find the crew of the *Packet* in a panic. As he climbed the stairs to the foredeck, he saw what the problem was. A French ship was skimming across the water towards them, its white sails billowing in the breeze.

"A privateer," yelled the captain, as he stared through his telescope. "She's armed to the gunwales. Let's try to outrun her."

Immediately the deck turned into a frenzy of activity as the sailors hoisted the sails and tightened the halyard while the captain tried to maneuver the *Packet* to take maximum advantage of the wind. Despite the crew's best efforts, the French ship continued to gain on them. They would soon be overrun.

Adoniram had read about the French privateers back in Boston. They were French ships whose crew had been given a license by the French government to plunder any enemy ships. In return for their license, the privateers turned over half the booty they stole to France. The practice of privateering

meant that private ships could act as a country's
navy, destroying and pillaging foreign ships at will.

Adoniram had no idea what the privateers
would do with him once they boarded the *Packet*,
but he knew this would be his last chance to retrieve
anything from his cabin. He raced down the deck
and descended the stairs two at a time. Reaching
his cabin, he yanked the door open and stood for a
moment looking around. What should he take with
him? His eyes fell on his desk. He thought he should
take his Bibles, all three of them—one in English, one
in Hebrew, and one in Latin. He quickly scooped
them up and shoved them into a cloth bag. Then
he remembered the letter Ann had written to him
just before he left Boston. He fumbled around in his
trunk until he found it.

Thump! Thump! Someone was whacking on his
door. Adoniram swiveled around to see two French
sailors glaring at him. He could smell stale alcohol
on their breath as they strode towards him.

Adoniram was surprised at how fast the French
privateers had overrun the *Packet*. He had been
below deck for only about three minutes, and in that
time they had taken complete control of the ship.
And since they controlled the ship it was pointless to
resist, so Adoniram allowed the privateers to push
him out the door and up the stairs onto the deck.

"Over there, you English dogs," yelled one of
the privateers in heavily accented English.

Adoniram was herded with the rest of the crew
to the starboard side of the ship, where they were

counted into groups of ten. The men were then forced to climb down a rope over the side of the *Packet* and into waiting longboats that ferried them to the *L'Invincible Napoleon*, the French privateer ship.

As Adoniram pitched with the motion of the longboat, he wondered what would happen next. Would he ever make it to London, or back to Boston, or would he be dumped at sea and left to drown? He felt for the letter from Ann inside his jacket pocket. With his hand on the letter, he comforted himself with the thought that at least if he was killed he would have died trying to become a missionary.

The privateers had no plan to kill Adoniram or the crew of the *Packet*. Instead, the men were thrown into the overcrowded, dark and dank hold of the French ship. They had no food, water, or chamber pots. A dull shaft of sunlight filtering through the dusty air of the hold was the only light the men had.

About three hours after the men had been brought aboard, Adoniram felt the *L'Invincible Napoleon* begin to move forward. They were under sail again. Adoniram wondered where they were headed. At the same time, the captain of the *Packet* finally took a roll call. Everyone was accounted for except the two Spanish passengers.

"I saw them being taken to a cabin," volunteered one crew member.

"That figures," grunted the captain. "The French have no war with the Spanish. They'll probably be treated like royalty, or at least a lot better than we will be."

[handwritten margin notes: TQ will he live?; CC why not kill them?; setting; wouldn't hurt Spanish]

[handwritten note at bottom: -X Kill (Spanish treated nicer bc no war w/ them)]

It didn't take long before Adoniram knew exactly what the captain meant. The rest of the day was a kind of living hell for him. A storm blew up, and stuck below water level with no fresh air, many of the sailors became violently ill. Adoniram was ill, too. Soon the hold was filled with the stench of vomit. Adoniram had lived a sparse life at Andover, but there had always been plenty of fresh well water to wash with, and he had taken great pains to keep himself and his clothes neat and clean. Now he could hardly stand the smell, and with nowhere for the sailors to relieve themselves, he braced himself for things to get a lot worse.

Days slipped by in the hold. The only high point was the visit by a French doctor, who held a perfumed handkerchief over his nose and mouth throughout the visit. Adoniram wanted desperately to tell the doctor that he was not one of the crew, that he was on his way to be a missionary, but he had no way to get through to him. Adoniram spoke no French, and the doctor spoke no English.

At first Adoniram could not believe what had happened to him. He questioned God as to why He had let it happen. After all, wasn't it important that he speak to the London Missionary Society as soon as possible? But as time went by, Adoniram began to accept the situation he was in. He decided that it was probably good preparation for missionary life, and he prayed for grace to ignore the stench around him. Soon he felt his old optimism returning, and he decided to put his time to good use. He found a spot just to the right of some boxes, where there was barely enough sunlight to read by, and set about reading his three Bibles. To keep his mind sharp he would read a chapter in Latin and then translate it into Hebrew. Then he would read the next chapter in Hebrew and translate it into Latin.

Adoniram was busy doing this one morning when the doctor climbed down the ladder into the hold. He watched as the doctor's eyes squinted to see what he was reading. The doctor picked up the two Bibles and tucked them under his arm. Adoniram wanted to protest, but he knew it was pointless. Any complaint was met with a whack from the stock of a musket. Instead, Adoniram sat and prayed that the doctor would return his precious Bibles. A few minutes later he did.

"So you speak Latin, my friend?" the doctor asked Adoniram in perfect Latin.

Adoniram's mouth fell open. In all his attempts to communicate with the doctor he had not thought of speaking Latin to him!

The two men had a long conversation, and Adoniram was able to explain that he was a pastor on his way to secure funds to become a missionary.

"I wish I had known sooner!" exclaimed the doctor when Adoniram was finished. "I will make arrangements for you to have your own cabin immediately."

Within an hour, Adoniram was hauled out of the hold and given water for a bath and his own cabin aboard the L'Invincible Napoleon. He ate dinner that night with the captain and the two Spanish passengers from the *Packet*, and although he could not understand what they were saying, he appreciated the good food and drink.

From then on he spent as much time up on deck as he could, enjoying the fresh air and the sun on his back. He understood from a crewman who spoke a little English that they were bound for Bayonne on the southwest coast of France.

One day, as he scanned the horizon, Adoniram's heart beat wildly. Perhaps he was not bound for France after all. What he saw was a large, well-armed brig flying the Union Jack. The brig spotted the *L'Invincible Napoleon* and gave chase. Adoniram watched as the French sailors scrambled to get their ship under more sail. The *L'Invincible Napoleon* was a smaller, more nimble ship that handled well in the water, and within an hour the British warship had fallen from sight. Adoniram's hopes of rescue were gone with it.

Adoniram did not spot any more British ships during the voyage, and eventually the *L'Invincible Napoleon* dropped anchor off Le Passage, Spain, where the two Spanish passengers were put ashore. Adoniram, however, had to stay aboard. As the ship sailed on to Bayonne, he marveled at the Pyrenees Mountains looming majestically above the horizon to the east. Soon the *L'Invincible Napoleon* was maneuvering its way into Bayonne Harbor.

Once the ship was tied up, the crew of the *Packet* were led out of the hold. By now they were filthy, and their eyes squinted against the bright sunlight. Adoniram wondered what would happen to him, since he wasn't a member of the crew. A gentle prod in the back with a bayonet gave him his answer.

"Over there, with the others," growled a sailor in French.

Adoniram had picked up a few words of the language by now, and he knew exactly what was expected of him. He joined the crew of the *Packet* as they were tied together with long ropes and marched down the gangplank and into the street below. He grimaced as he stood between the cook and one of the helmsmen from the *Packet*. The rancid odor of the men's unwashed bodies made him gag.

"Faster, faster," yelled the sailor with the bayonet. Adoniram felt the tug of the rope in front of him, and he walked forward into the surging crowd, which parted for them. The people jeered and spat on the English prisoners. Adoniram knew he had to do something, but what? He was in a strange country, roped to two other men and being marched off to prison. Recalling every bit of French he had learned aboard the *L'Invincible Napoleon*, he began to shout to the passers-by, telling them, or so he thought, that he was an American citizen and should be freed at once.

Adoniram's words had an unusual effect on the crowd, who went wild when they heard them, slapping their sides and laughing until the tears rolled down their cheeks. After several minutes of this, Adoniram began to think he was using the wrong words and that he was doing more harm than good. So he decided to switch to English. "This is an outrage," he yelled in his booming voice. "I am a citizen of a country that is not at war with you. How dare you capture me on the high seas and bring me here against my will. I demand to see a judge at once."

One of the guards leading the prisoners raised his pistol and threatened to beat Adoniram with it, but Adoniram kept on yelling. More than anything, Adoniram knew that if he ended up in prison with the British sailors, it could be years before he saw sunlight and freedom again. Ann was waiting to marry him when he got back to Boston, and the American Board was counting on him to secure the money needed for the first American missionaries to be sent out. But most of all, the people of Burma needed to hear the gospel. Adoniram could not allow himself to go to prison. He raised his voice and shouted some more.

cc

cc

- Ad. Angry = yelled French
- Ann was going to marry him in Boston
- Board counted on him to get $$

Chapter 7

The Stranger

B e quiet," a low male voice came from the crowd. "Be quiet or they'll blow your head off."

Adoniram stopped yelling long enough to look around. Who had spoken to him in English?

"Over here," the voice came again.

Adoniram turned and stared into the face of an American military officer.

New Person "What's your name?" the officer asked Adoniram as he walked along keeping pace with the prisoners. "What are you doing here?"

Now that Adoniram had found someone to listen to him, he lowered his voice and quickly told his story to the military officer.

"I'll try to help. Be patient," the officer said as he faded into the jeering crowd. *!! Hope*

o American military officer offers help to Adoniram

71

Now as Adoniram marched along the cobble-stone street he had some hope. An American man out there knew who he was and that he needed help. But would it be enough? Would the man really go out of his way to help a stranger? Adoniram would have to wait and see.

When the prisoners from the *Packet* finally reached the prison, they were thrown into a dungeon. As he sat with his back against a damp, moss-covered brick wall, Adoniram prayed that the stranger would not forget him.

Several hours passed. Adoniram guessed it was about seven o'clock at night—though he had no way of knowing for sure—when the door to the dungeon creaked open. Framed against the oil light in the hallway was the stranger, wearing a billowing military cloak. He spoke in French to the jailer, who stepped forward and grabbed a lamp off a hook on the wall. The jailer grunted as he handed the lamp to the stranger.

Adoniram sat silently, hugging his knees and watching every move. The stranger walked slowly around the cell, shining the lamp up to the faces of the prisoners. "Non," he said as he peered at each face. When he came to Adoniram, he held up the lamp briefly and again said, "Non."

The jailer spoke a few sentences in French. The stranger nodded and turned to hang the lamp back on the hook on the wall. As he did so, he swirled his cloak around Adoniram.

Adoniram felt the cloak enfold him, and in a flash he understood the stranger's daring plan. He crouched beneath the cloak and clasped his arms around the man's waist. He felt the man begin to walk, and Adoniram matched his footsteps. As they "walked" out of the dungeon, Adoniram heard the wooden door thump shut behind them, and then he heard the clink of coins being handed over. "Just a bit farther," he heard the American military officer whisper.

Half squatting, half standing under the huge cloak, Adoniram walked step for step with the stranger to the front of the prison, where more money was handed over. Then, with the clang of the metal gate behind him, Adoniram knew he was out in the open street. The American man whipped the cloak off him and whispered "Follow me" as he set off running down the street. Adoniram followed the man through the darkness until they reached the docks.

"Over here," the stranger said. "Quickly, they have the gangplank lowered for us."

The two men sprinted up the gangplank and onto the deck of a sloop.

"You'll be safe here," the American officer said. "I've made arrangements for the captain to hide you. Get out of France as soon as you can." With that the man turned and hurried off back the way he had come.

Adoniram stood on the deck, breathless and amazed. Less than an hour ago he had been in a dark, damp dungeon. Now he was aboard a ship, staring up at a starry night! And what was more, he had no idea who the man was or why he had helped him.

It took Adoniram until May, four months after setting sail from Boston, to finally reach London. Nevertheless, Adoniram was pleased to learn he had arrived at a good time. The governing board of the London Missionary Society was about to hold its annual meeting, and it was happy to allow Adoniram time to present the American Board's case for support directly to the board. Also, a letter of encouragement from the American Board, plus money for the passage home, was waiting for the young missionary-to-be.

Adoniram immediately sent a letter of thanks back to the American Board. Then he set about preparing his presentation. It was not until he was actually repeating what he had been sent to say that he realized just how unlikely it was that his proposal would be accepted. Basically, he was telling the London Missionary Society that four young, inexperienced American men would like to be sent out as American missionaries. However, Adoniram explained, since they had no money and it seemed unlikely they could raise it, they wanted the London Missionary Society to sponsor them while leaving the control of where they went and what they did there in the hands of the American Board.

The members of the governing board of the London Missionary Society (LMS) listened politely to what Adoniram had to say. When he was done, they told him that while they admired his enthusiasm, there was no way the London Missionary Society was going to pass over English missionaries to sponsor foreigners over whom they would have little or no authority. Adoniram could see their point, and he began to think of an alternate plan. More than anything he wanted to get to the mission field, and he didn't much care who sponsored him. So he asked the London Missionary Society if they would send him and the three other missionary candidates out as LMS missionaries and not involve the American Board. He argued that it was more important for him to go than to be officially known as an American missionary. After some discussion, the London Missionary Society agreed to the request. If the other three missionary candidates agreed, the LMS would send all four of them out, and the American Board would have to find some other way to support the missionaries it wanted to send out.

Adoniram had what he wanted as he boarded the *Augustus* in June 1811, bound for New York City. He had found a way to get himself and his three friends to East Asia as missionaries. Yet he couldn't help feeling disappointed that in all the United States there was not enough interest in missions to be able to sponsor four missionaries.

When he reached New York, Adoniram was tempted to catch a stagecoach straight back to Massachusetts, but something had bothered him on the voyage home, something he had to take care of before he went one step farther.

The last time he had been in New York was three years earlier, when he had joined up with a group of swindlers masquerading as a troop of actors. Now it was time to pay back all the people he had cheated during that time. He told himself there was no point in being a missionary if he left unpaid debts at home. It took him three days to track down all the innkeepers he owed money to, and much to their surprise, he paid each one of them back. When he had finished, his conscience was clear and he felt free to go home.

Some encouraging news was waiting for Adoniram when he finally got back to Massachusetts. Mr. Norris, who had helped pay Adoniram's passage to London, had from the start been a strong supporter of the idea to send out American foreign missionaries. He had died while Adoniram was away, and he had left thirty thousand dollars to the American Board.

"Thirty thousand dollars!" gasped Adoniram when he heard the news. "That's more than enough to send out four missionaries and their wives. We will be able to go out with the American Board after all."

Adoniram wished he could start planning right away with Samuel Newell and Gordon Hall, but they were both in Philadelphia studying medicine as a way to better prepare themselves for missionary work. The four missionaries-to-be had decided to make their way to India and from there see what missionary opportunities awaited them in the Far

East. Of course, there was no doubt in Adoniram's mind as to where he was headed. God was calling him to Burma.

Adoniram also had something else he wanted to discuss with Samuel Newell. While Adoniram had been away, Samuel had become engaged to one of Ann's closest friends, seventeen-year-old Harriet Atwood. Ann was very excited about the idea, because now she would have someone to discuss "female" things with on the mission field. Adoniram wasn't so sure it was a good idea, though. Harriet was a slightly built young woman who had previously suffered from tuberculosis. To him she looked as though a good puff of ocean breeze would blow her right off the deck of the ship! He wondered how she would even survive a sea voyage to India, let alone worry about what lay ahead at the other end.

Time began to drag for Adoniram, who was eager to be on his way. But John Norris's will had been contested by some members of his family, and although it seemed certain the American Board would prevail in court and get the money promised it, it all took time. To make matters worse, the newspapers were reporting that the United States was about to go to war with England. When that happened, all merchant shipping would stop. After reading this, leaving became a matter of urgency for Adoniram, who felt that if he didn't go now, he might never go. After several days of discussions with the slow-moving missions board, it was finally agreed that until the inheritance was made available, the board should seek some other way to raise the money the missionaries would need.

AB

The minutes of the meeting of the American Board that day recorded, "Messrs. Adoniram Judson Jr., Samuel Nott Jr., Samuel Newell, and Gordon Hall were appointed missionaries to labor under the direction of this board in Asia, either in the Burman Empire, or in Surat, or in Prince of Wales Island, or elsewhere, as in view of the Prudential Committee, Providence shall open by the most favorable door."

$$
↓↓
trip

At the same meeting it was also decided that the missionaries should be allotted $666.66 a year if they were married and $444.45 if they were single, plus the same amount to equip themselves to go and $300 extra for books. It was a generous amount of money to offer. Of course, outside of waiting for the money from Mr. Norris's will, no one knew where the allotments would come from.

↓!
Hope
↓
Harmony

As 1811 rolled on and the vibrant colors of fall gave way to a particularly harsh winter, Adoniram became more concerned about the war brewing between England and the United States. Already New York harbor was under a British blockade. Finally, in mid-January 1812, a message reached Adoniram. Samuel Newell had located a ship, the *Harmony*, which was headed from Philadelphia to Calcutta, India, and the captain had permission to transport the missionaries to India. Adoniram and Ann raced into action. This was the opportunity they had been waiting for, and they both knew it might be the last ship leaving American waters for a very long time.

Adoniram made a rushed trip home to Plymouth to say good-bye to his parents and to Abigail and Elnathan. It was a difficult time for them all. His family was convinced they would never see him again. Early on Monday morning, February 3, 1812, Adoniram said a final good-bye to his parents and Abigail before mounting his horse to ride back to Bradford. Eighteen-year-old Elnathan accompanied his older brother as far as Boston before wishing him well and turning his horse around to head back home. Adoniram rode on alone through thick snow to Bradford to meet with Ann.

It was time to get married—quickly. A crowd joined twenty-three-year-old Adoniram and twenty-two-year-old Ann as they exchanged wedding vows on Wednesday, February 5, 1812. The ceremony was held in the Hasseltines' west living room, the same room where Ann and Adoniram had first laid eyes on each other twenty months before. Samuel Newell was there, too, with Harriet. They were due to be married the following week. Samuel Nott was also in attendance with his fiancee, Roxana.

The following day, February 6, a special service was held at Tabernacle Church in Salem to officially send off the missionaries headed for India. There were now five men, since Luther Rice had joined the group. Over two thousand people attended the service, many of them setting out before dawn to walk to the church. It was the coldest day of the year, but the number of people packed into the church made it as warm as summer inside.

Several days after the service, more good news arrived. A second ship, a small brig named the *Caravan*, lay at anchor in Salem Harbor. It was about to set sail for Calcutta, India, and the captain was willing to transport the missionaries. With this news, it was decided that the group should split up so that if one of the ships was lost at sea or overrun by privateers, at least half the missionaries would make it to their destination. Samuel Nott and his new wife, Roxana, along with Gordon Hall and Luther Rice, would head for Philadelphia to sail aboard the *Harmony*, while Samuel Newell and his new wife, Harriet, and Adoniram and Ann would sail aboard the *Caravan*.

Before the Newells and the Judsons could set sail, the worst storm in years hit the northern coast of Massachusetts, dumping several feet of snow across the area. The *Caravan* was forced to lay at anchor off the end of Crowninshield's Wharf. It was too small to brave the fierce seas whipped up by the storm. One day went by, and then another, as the two missionary couples waited patiently. Adoniram busied himself preaching and talking about missions wherever he could find an audience. The results of his efforts stunned him. When he had first heard that the *Caravan* was available to transport them to India, the American Board had only twelve hundred dollars in the bank. As a result of

[handwritten margin notes: "Raised an extra 5k", "Gods delays can be good delays.", "wait"]

his speaking engagements, Adoniram had raised an extra five thousand dollars. It was more than enough money to send the missionaries out with a year's pay in advance without having to rely on the money that would be coming from Mr. Norris's will.

One delay followed another as the anxious missionaries waited for the *Caravan* to set sail. First it was the weather, and then the captain informed them that he needed to wait for some special cargo to arrive. Finally, on February 18, Adoniram received word that it was time to board the ship. They would be sailing with the high tide the following morning. Adoniram took their last pieces of baggage down to the dock, leaving Ann to say good-bye to several of her friends who had gathered.

[handwritten margin note: "Feb 18 could sail"]

When Adoniram returned, the house where they were staying was filled with well-wishers. Adoniram marveled at the way his new wife could make a party out of anything. There was just one problem with this party: Ann didn't understand the dread her husband felt over saying good-bye. Adoniram braced himself as he stepped inside the house, but he couldn't bear it. Quietly he slipped out, leaving a note for Ann saying he would meet her aboard ship. When Ann read the note, she was very upset. There were many things she did not understand about her new husband. Still, she graciously said good-bye to all her friends and accepted a sleighride down to the dock.

[handwritten margin notes: "setting", "!! can't bear to leave"]

Sure enough, Adoniram was standing on the icy deck of the *Caravan* waiting for Ann. He clambered onto the dock and took his wife's hand and guided her up the gangplank and onto the ship, which was now tied up alongside Crowninshield's Wharf. "I'm sorry," he said. "I can take only so many good-byes."

Ann nodded as she climbed aboard the ship. Adoniram squeezed her hand gently as a sign of thanks. He also knew how brave it was for his wife to board any ship, since her only brother had been drowned in a shipwreck only months before. As a result of the incident, Ann had developed a great fear of drowning.

Early the next morning Adoniram and Ann stood together on deck as the *Caravan* slipped out into the open harbor. The last time Adoniram had sailed aboard a ship he had been kidnapped and imprisoned. He hoped that he and Ann would not meet the same fate. But the truth was, the *Caravan* was a much more lucrative prize than the *Packet*. Thinking his ship would be the last vessel to leave Salem for India before the British blockaded the harbor, Captain Heard had loaded up his ship with forty thousand dollars' worth of trading goods. And not only that, he had confided to Adoniram that there was two thousand dollars in silver coins in the ship's safe. All of this weighed on Adoniram. If the *Caravan* was boarded by privateers or pirates, this time he would have a wife to worry about and keep safe.

"God," he prayed, as the *Caravan* headed towards open sea, "may we all live to see India."

Chapter 8

Passage to India

Five days after setting sail from Salem, Adoniram anxiously paced the deck of the *Caravan*, praying as he walked. Things were not going well. Ann and Harriet were both violently ill below deck, which, given the situation, Adoniram decided was a good thing. At least he wouldn't need to tell them right away that the ship had sprung a leak. Unless the desperate crew moved enough cargo in the hold to uncover it, the *Caravan* could well sink before the day was out. Even the pigs penned on the starboard side of the ship seemed to sense that danger was near. They squealed loudly and pushed at the flimsy gate that held them captive.

"All hands to the pumps," the captain bellowed. Two sailors scurried down from the rigging and ran

[handwritten margin notes: "Ann & Harriet = sick" and "!! Leak"]

past Adoniram, who followed them as they disappeared down a hatchway into the dingy bowels of the ship. Two feet of water was sloshing around in the bottom of the hold.

"Over here," yelled the first mate. "I've found the leak. It's a gusher. We're going to need a bucket of pitch. In the meantime, keep pumping, you lot," he told the sailors manning the bilge pumps.

Water was pouring in between two of the planks in the ship's hull. Gently, using a knife and a hammer, the first mate jammed some pieces of hemp rope into the gap. The flow of water into the ship slowed. As the first mate jammed the rope farther and farther into the hole, the flow was almost completely stemmed. Soon a sailor arrived with a bucket of hot pitch. The first mate worked the black goo down into the crack on top of the rope, making sure he used as much of it as possible. As the pitch cooled, it hardened into a permanent seal over the hole. Soon the sailors had the water pumped out of the *Caravan*'s hold, and the ship was no longer in danger of sinking. At least not from that hole.

After the excitement of the leak, things began to settle into a steady routine for the missionaries. Ann and Harriet felt better and were able to join the men in the mornings for Bible study and prayer. They all ate lunch with the captain and then did their "exercise." On his ill-fated trip to England, Adoniram had walked the decks of the *Packet* for exercise. But the *Caravan* was a particularly small vessel—only two hundred sixty feet long—and walking her

decks was tedious and uninvigorating. To solve th
problem, Ann mischievously opened her bag one
morning and pulled out two jump ropes. Handing
one to Adoniram, she laughed. "Here, I bet I can
skip without stopping longer than you can!"

Adoniram broke into loud peals of laughter as
he took the rope from his wife. He loved the way
Ann was so full of life. The rope skipping turned
out to be good exercise, and Samuel Newell often
skipped with them, but not Harriet. After finally
adjusting to the constant motion of the ship, she
had become sick for another reason: <u>She was pregnant. The baby was expected to arrive in November</u>
and, if all went well, in India.

The weeks slipped by, and as the ship moved
south, the weather became <u>hotter and the voyage
more monotonous</u>. Once a week the cook ordered a
pig or some chickens killed so there would be fresh
meat to eat. Water, though, was rationed because
Captain Heard didn't expect to put in to any ports
along the way. As far as he was concerned, the less
contact they had with others, the less chance they
had of being robbed. Occasionally they spotted
another ship on the horizon, but the captain would
always steer the *Caravan* away from it.

During the voyage Adoniram had plenty of
time for the work he loved—<u>Bible translation</u>. He
was attempting his own translation of the New
Testament from Greek into English, and he had
many interesting discussions with Samuel Newell
over the exact meaning of the original words. One

Baby arrive in Nov.

word particularly interested him, though he had no idea how thinking about that one word would change his entire life. It was the word *baptism*. Adoniram had been born and raised a member of the Congregational church, which taught that babies should be baptized soon after they were born by being sprinkled with water. Adoniram had been baptized that way himself, and he had always expected to baptize his children in the same manner. But aboard the *Caravan*, somewhere near the equator, he was coming to a disturbing conclusion. As he studied the meaning of the Greek word for baptism, he discovered that it never meant "to sprinkle." Rather, it was used to convey the way that Christians in the Bible were immersed into the water in rivers and lakes to be baptized.

This was quite a problem for Adoniram. He was one of the first group of Congregational missionaries ever to be sent out from America, and even before he had arrived at his destination he was having doubts about whether the way his church carried out baptisms was correct. He discussed it with Ann, who at first laughed at him. But when Ann realized how the issue was playing on her husband's mind, she tried to reason with him. But Adoniram continued to worry. What should he do after he had converted non-Christians in Burma? Should he sprinkle them with water or take them to the river and immerse them as the Baptists did? He had no answer, but Ann did. She was a strict Congregationalist, all her family and friends were

Congregationalists, and the people who had sponsored their voyage were Congregationalists. Whatever Adoniram decided to do was his business, but she informed him there was no way she was ever going to desert her denomination.

Finally, on June 12, 1812, one hundred fourteen days after setting sail from Salem, Massachusetts, they finally sighted land. According to Captain Heard, they were off the coast of Orissa, India, and the mountains in the distance were the Golcondas. They sailed on up the Bay of Bengal towards Calcutta, edging closer to the coastline as they did so. Adoniram and Ann Judson and Samuel and Harriet Newell were fascinated by what they saw from the deck of the ship. Banana palms laden with bunches of bananas grew near the water's edge. Bananas were a rare and expensive fruit in New England. In fact, none of the four missionaries had ever eaten one, and it amazed them to see so many of them just growing wild. As night fell the following day, the *Caravan* dropped anchor near the mouth of the Hooghly River at the northern end of the Bay of Bengal. There they waited for a pilot to come aboard and guide the ship through the treacherous shallow waters of the river mouth and then on up to Calcutta.

The following morning the pilot arrived and began the careful task of maneuvering the *Caravan* up the Hooghly River, a channel in the Ganges River delta. The four missionaries stayed on deck the whole time, excited to see their first glimpses of Indian people going about their daily activities. They watched as the ship sailed past brilliant green rice paddies. They observed fishermen casting their nets from the water's edge and women walking along with enormous baskets balanced on their heads. Adoniram tried to take in every detail. He thanked God he had lived long enough to finally see the mission field.

At three o'clock the following day they reached Calcutta, and as they docked, Adoniram scanned the rows of ships looking for any sign of the *Harmony*. He had no idea whether they had reached India first, or whether the Notts, Gordon Hall, and Luther Rice would be waiting to meet them when they docked.

"No sign of the *Harmony*," said Captain Heard, as if reading Adoniram's thoughts. "Still, we can make inquiries when we get to the police station to register your presence. There'll be all kinds of trouble if I don't do that first. The East India Company is very particular about keeping track of all foreigners in India."

When the *Caravan* was finally tied up alongside the dock in Calcutta, Adoniram went to find Samuel Newell so that the two of them could accompany Captain Heard to the police station. In the Newells' cabin he found Ann and Harriet gorging themselves on bananas and pineapples.

"These taste wonderful," said Ann, holding out half a plump banana for Adoniram to try. "This yellow fruit is a pineapple. It's so sweet," she added, pointing to the cut-up chunks of juicy yellow fruit on the table.

Adoniram laughed. He was happy, he was in India, and he knew his wife was going to enjoy the challenges that lay ahead of them.

An hour later, though, he was not so happy. The clerk at the police station had been rude and uninterested in their case. He had told them it was foolish to land in Calcutta without written permission from the directors of the East India Company. They ran things in India, and no one could stay without their permission. Adoniram knew this was true for the British, but since he was an American he had assumed the rules would be different for him. He told the clerk so.

"You Americans!" the clerk snorted with indignation. "You have no regard for rules, do you? Well, I can tell you this. I doubt you'll get permission to stay here. All I can do for you is to give you a certificate to say you've reported here and pass the whole case on to the East India Company." With that he stamped some papers and handed them to Adoniram and Samuel.

Dejected, the two men left the police station. As they did so, Adoniram pulled a piece of paper from his jacket pocket. "I was wondering if Fort William College is close by," he asked Captain Heard. "I would like to visit Dr. Carey."

"It's about a mile away," replied the captain. "And I hope you get a warmer welcome there than you got at the police station. Come on, I'll show you the way."

Captain Heard led the way through a maze of densely populated streets to Fort William College. William Carey was working in his office. He invited Adoniram and Samuel in while Captain Heard returned to his ship to oversee the unloading of the *Caravan*'s cargo. William Carey was a short, bald man, but he had an enormous reputation, and Adoniram felt honored to meet him at last. He knew of Carey's humble start in life as a shoemaker back in England. Despite his lowly start, through sheer determination Carey had opened the eyes of English Christians to the need to send out missionaries. He had founded the Baptist Missionary Society and gone out as the organization's first missionary. His extraordinary ability translating foreign languages had earned him the position of professor of Oriental languages at Fort William College. Of course, Carey also continued his missions work, using his college salary to help support a large missionary community at Serampore, farther up the Hooghly River.

More than anything, Adoniram wanted to learn all that William Carey might know about missionary work in Burma. But the news was not good. Carey's son Felix lived in Rangoon, Burma, but he was allowed to do so only because he was married to a Burmese woman. He was forbidden to do missionary work, and the penalty for disobeying was death.

Adoniram gulped hard when he heard this. "That sounds a little harsh," he said.

• William Carey - William College
• Ad wanted to learn more about missions

William Carey nodded. "It does, but many people in Burma wake up each morning not knowing whether they will be alive by evening. <u>Almost</u> !! <u>any offense carries a terrible punishment</u>. A man Ad. could have boiling lead poured down his throat for nas chewing opium. Only three months ago a Burmese to be commander ordered that five hundred of his men careful be buried alive because they were new recruits and no one had yet told them all the rules. <u>Burma is a</u> < setting <u>place in great need of the gospel. There are fifteen</u> <u>million people living there, and they have not one</u> <u>Bible in their own language. But the king has no</u> intention of letting any foreigners gain a foothold. It is a noble goal of yours to go to Burma, though perhaps not one that is obtainable. But," concluded William Carey, stroking his chin, "you'll have long enough to think about where you should go from here. The important thing is to get permission to stay until your friends arrive. I will do all I can to help. In the meantime, you are welcome to come to <u>Serampore</u>. We would all like to get to know you and your wives better." Place

With the help of William Carey, Adoniram and Samuel were able to get temporary permits that allowed them to stay in India for the time being. Finally, the missionaries said good-bye to Captain Heard, who had been so kind to them throughout the voyage <u>from Salem</u>. They loaded themselves into a small boat and set off upriver to <u>Serampore</u>, the Danish-controlled enclave William Carey had <u>fled to when the East India Company had tried to</u> expel him from India.

William Ward &
Joshua Marshman.

What Adoniram saw on his arrival in Serampore
astonished him. There on the banks of the Hooghly
River sat a large Christian community. William
Carey's two associates, William Ward and Joshua
Marshman, showed the group around. One of the
centerpieces of the compound was a large print
shop, complete with its own papermaking equip-
ment. As the men walked, they passed a burned-
out building that Joshua Marshman explained had
been destroyed in a fire several months before.
"The building housed the translation rooms and
was where the type was set. A lot was lost in the
fire, but Dr. Carey is not a man to give up easily.
We have already begun the translation work again,
and plans are being drawn up for a new building."

The Judsons and the Newells had been guests at
Serampore for two weeks when, on July 1, the men
were summoned to the police station in Calcutta.
The news was every bit as bad as they dreaded it
would be. The East India Company had decided
to brand them "undesirables" and had ordered
Captain Heard to return all four of them to the
United States. To make sure the captain did so, no
port clearance would be given to him unless the
four missionaries were onboard his ship.

Adoniram was devastated by the news. He
wondered what he should do next. The *Harmony*
had not yet arrived, and how could he ever explain
having to return to America? Arriving home on the
same ship he'd left on could spell the end to any
future American missions. He had hoped to be the

!! to go back - EIC

I missionaries have to go back - EIC

TQ

- Forced to head near French Isle by EIC
- bw - Newells left w/ unborn child

first of many successes, not the first failed American missionary.

Thoughts swirled though Adoniram's mind as he returned to Serampore. He had come so far, but where could he go now? Burma sounded out of the question, as did any other British-controlled area. The officer of the East India Company had made that very plain at the police station. There was one missionary in China, Robert Morrison, but he was officially recognized as a translator. If it became known he was a Christian, or if other missionaries joined him, he would be put to death. Then there were Arabia, Turkey, and Persia, but the Moslem rulers there had made it clear that death awaited all Christians who came ashore to convert others to their religion.

Many of Adoniram and Ann's new friends in Calcutta and Serampore urged the couple to return to the United States and become missionaries to the American Indians in the uncharted territories west of the Mississippi River. But Adoniram's heart was not there. He told himself that if William Carey would not give up after such a destructive fire, then neither would he. He would find a mission field in East Asia, or he would die trying.

Captain Heard was not due to set sail again for at least six weeks, which gave the missionaries a little more time in India to try to come up with a plan. Joshua Marshman from the Serampore mission made a trip to Calcutta to see what he could do about the situation. Eventually, he was able to prevail with his contacts in the East India Company, and he was unofficially told that the missionaries would be allowed to find passage on another ship as long as they headed for the Isle of France (today called Mauritius) in the western Indian Ocean and away from East India Company-controlled territory.

!!
All can't board ship

A ship, the _Col. Gillespie,_ was found. It was about to set sail for the Isle of France, but it had room for only two passengers. Harriet Newell's baby was due in just three months, and it was decided that Harriet and Samuel should be the ones to make the trip. That way they could get themselves established in the Isle of France before the baby arrived.

Harriet & Samuel left 4 France w/ unborn child

Adoniram and Ann stood watching the Newells disappear down the Hooghly River aboard the _Col. Gillespie._ Ann yelled a final word to her childhood friend. "God bless you, Harriet. We'll all meet in the Isle of France as soon as we can find a ship. Wait for us."

Adoniram waved, too, and he hoped all would be well when they met again.

Four days after the Newells left for the Isle of France, the _Harmony_ finally docked in Calcutta. The ship had not been boarded by privateers or sunk in a storm after all, but she had encountered unfavorable winds in the Bay of Bengal. Adoniram and Ann had a wonderful reunion with Samuel and Roxana Nott, Gordon Hall, and Luther Rice. The friends had not seen each other since their official send-off service in Salem, Massachusetts, seven months before.

Now they were all safely together in India. But they didn't have long together there. If the East India Company had been unhappy about the Judsons and the Newells being in India, they were furious when four more American missionaries arrived. In fact, within days of the *Harmony*'s arrival, the missionaries were informed that they were all being deported to England in a convoy of ships that would soon be setting sail from Calcutta. Adoniram knew they had to do something, and fast.

Chapter 9

Don't Throw Your Life Away

Getting out of Calcutta proved more difficult than Adoniram had imagined. The missionaries played a cat-and-mouse game with the East India Company, always trying to stay one step ahead. The Notts and Gordon Hall had finally managed to book passage on a ship and sneak out of Calcutta without being detected by East India Company officials. They headed for the island of Ceylon off the southeast tip of India where they hoped to establish a mission station.

Adoniram and Ann and Luther Rice tried to do the same aboard the *Créole*. However, the East India Company got wind of their plan and sent word after the ship, ordering the pilot to drop anchor in the Hooghly River and wait for the police to come

[handwritten margin notes: CC ; !! ; can get out of Cal. w/o getting detected ; Notts & Hall ; !! ; Got caught ; Ad., Ann, & Rice]

97

and search the vessel. The missionaries were forced to flee to the safety of shore. They made one last desperate attempt to convince officials in Calcutta that they should be issued a permit to sail to the Isle of France instead of being deported to England. Miraculously, this time a permit for them to leave was issued, and quickly they hired a boat and raced off downriver to try to catch up to the *Créole*. They found her lying at anchor off Saugar in the mouth of the Hooghly River, waiting for two crew members to arrive before setting out across the Bay of Bengal.

It was now January 17, 1813, and the *Créole* was within sight of Port Louis on the Isle of France. It had been seven weeks since the missionaries had clambered aboard the ship at Saugar. For much of the voyage they just rested trying to recover from their harrowing six-month stay in India. Adoniram was amazed at how much energy it had taken trying to stay one step ahead of East India Company officials. And then there had been the big change. Staying at Serampore with Baptist missionaries had convinced Adoniram that the Baptists were right and he needed to be baptized their way himself. Much to his surprise and delight, Ann had been studying the issues herself and agreed with him. Together they had been baptized by William Ward.

William Carey and the other missionaries at Serampore had been careful not to try to influence Adoniram or Ann in any way. If they were Congregationalists, that was fine for them. But once the Judsons decided they wanted to be baptized by full immersion, the Baptist missionaries tried to support them in every way they could. They even offered to fund Adoniram and Ann's missionary work for a year while they waited to hear whether the American Baptists would accept them as their missionaries. William Carey himself had written a letter to Baptist leaders in the United States commending Adoniram and asking that he and Ann be accepted as their first foreign missionaries. When they left Calcutta, Adoniram and Ann had not yet received a reply from the American Baptists.

"I wonder what Harriet will say about our no longer being Congregationalists," pondered Ann as the buildings of Port Louis came into view. "Do you think she will mind?" she asked Adoniram.

"I doubt it, Ann. You two have been best friends for years. I'm sure Harriet will get over it. And although we won't be able to work in the same mission, I'm hopeful we will be close enough so you can see her often."

"And the baby," interjected Ann. "I can't wait to see the baby. It must be two months old by now. I wonder whether it's a boy or a girl. And what did they name it?" Her eyes danced with anticipation.

"Here comes a boat alongside now. Perhaps it will have some news," said Adoniram.

"Look! It's Samuel," said Ann, racing to the side of the ship. "Thank goodness, I won't have to wait a moment longer for news."

Adoniram and Ann waited together as Samuel Newell clambered up the rope ladder and onto the deck of the _Créole_. Samuel looked pale and was unsteady on his feet.

"Come and sit down in our cabin," offered Ann once they had greeted each other. "Was the boat ride out rough?"

Samuel shook his head, and Adoniram noticed tears forming in the corners of his eyes. Ann put her hand on Samuel's arm. "What is it? Is everything all right? Are Harriet and the baby well?"

Once again Samuel shook his head. "Dead," he said in a low whisper. "Both of them are dead."

Ann gasped, her hands pressed tightly over her mouth to suppress a cry.

Somehow Adoniram escorted them both to the cabin, where the facts came out. The _Col. Gillespie_, the ship on which the Newells had sailed, had sprung a leak and was forced to put into a small harbor for repairs. The repairs took two weeks, after which time they set sail again. But the winds were against them most of the way, and the ship made slow progress, so slow, in fact, that the time arrived for Harriet to have the baby. Lying on the cabin floor with only Samuel at her side, she had delivered a little girl. All went well, until the next day when they encountered a bad storm. Everything and everyone aboard the _Col. Gillespie_ were soaked. The following day, Harriet's nineteenth birthday, the baby became ill with pneumonia and died five days later. By then Harriet herself had become ill. The delivery of the baby and the damp conditions had combined with the symptoms of her tuberculosis to make her very weak. She thought constantly about her baby and longed to be in heaven with her. In the middle of November she got her wish, and Samuel Newell had buried her under a tree in the Port Louis cemetery.

The deaths stunned Adoniram and Ann, especially since Ann had just learned she was expecting a baby herself. What might go wrong with her pregnancy? Things seemed to have a way of turning out differently than expected.

The governor of the Isle of France was very kind to the missionaries, but Adoniram soon found out that because of the deplorable state of slavery, it was pointless to stay on the island. <u>Almost the entire population of the Isle of France was enslaved to wealthy plantation owners.</u> These slave owners forbid their slaves to practice any form of religion and forbid missionaries to preach to them. It was a strange situation. The island was filled with people in need of the gospel, but there was no opportunity to preach it to them or convert them.

After several weeks, Samuel Newell had recovered enough from the shock of his wife's death to start thinking about what to do next. While he respected Adoniram's decision to become a Baptist, he was still a Congregationalist and decided to head to Ceylon to try to track down Samuel and Roxana Nott and Gordon Hall and participate in the missionary work they were doing. Luther Rice did not stay long on the Isle of France, either. He had become ill with liver problems, and the doctor had told him he that if he didn't find a cooler climate to live in he would surely die. Luther had also become a Baptist in Serampore, and he decided to return to the United States to help raise support among the American Baptists for the Judsons. He left on the first available ship, and soon Adoniram and Ann found themselves alone on the island.

After several weeks of soul searching, the Judsons decided to head for Penang in the Straits of Malacca on the other side of the Indian Ocean. They would have to get there in two stages. First they would have to find a ship to take them to Madras, India, and once there, they would need to find another ship to take them on to Penang. They left Port Louis on May 7, 1813, aboard the *Countess of Harcourt*. A month later they arrived in Madras on the east coast of India.

In Madras they were hosted by two British missionaries. It was not long, however, before officials of the East India Company were on Adoniram's trail again. He needed to find a ship bound for Penang, and quickly. Leaving Ann, now very pregnant, in the care of the missionaries, he set out for the docks each morning hoping to find some way to get to Penang. He did not find what he was looking for, and after a week he received word that the police were preparing to arrest him and Ann and deport them to England. He began desperately looking for a ship that would take them anywhere but to England.

Adoniram finally found a ship, the *Georgiana*, which was due to set sail the following day. The ship was a Portuguese vessel, and her name was a lot grander than her appearance. She was dilap-idated, and she listed to starboard. But she was afloat and was scheduled to leave the next morning. That was a lot more important to Adoniram than her appearance.

"Where is she bound?" he asked the shipping agent, not much caring whether it was Penang or Madagascar.

"Rangoon, Burma," came the reply.

For once Adoniram was speechless. What should he do? He hurried back to Ann and laid out the choices for her. If they stayed one more day in Madras, they would be arrested and sent to England. Or they could board the *Georgiana*, as unseaworthy as she was, and sail to one of the most inhospitable places on earth, a place that every missionary they had met so far had warned them against going to. Finally Adoniram took his wife's hand. "You have a baby coming. What do you think we should do?" he asked.

Tears welled in Ann's eyes. "If we go to England, the baby will be born onboard ship, like Harriet's," she said. "And even if we go to Burma, the baby might still come before we get there. I don't know, Adoniram. You will have to decide what God is calling us to do."

Adoniram tried to discuss with his new missionary friends in Madras what to do, but there was no room for discussion. Everyone had the same advice. "Don't throw your life away in Burma. Go to England. Make your way back to the East and

Handwritten margin notes: TQ — "Would they risk going to Madras & getting caught?"; "!! Ann = scared / trusts God"

Handwritten at bottom: dilapidated

set up a mission station somewhere where you are welcomed."

TQ

This made sense to Adoniram, and he would have followed their advice except for one thing: He could not get rid of the thought that God had set up circumstances in such a way as to get him and Ann to Burma.

!!

June 22, 1813

And so it was that on June 22, 1813, the Judsons boarded the *Georgiana*, bound for Burma. With them was an Englishwoman they had hired to help Ann with the baby's birth and to look after the baby once it arrived. The woman seemed strong and healthy, and Ann looked forward to the help and companionship she would provide. Within hours of the *Georgiana*'s setting sail, however, the woman fell to the deck writhing and groaning. Adoniram and Ann rushed to her side to help, but there was nothing they could do. The woman was already dead.

!!
cc

Death shocked them

The Judsons were shocked by the turn of events. Was death to follow them everywhere they went? Adoniram also worried about Ann, who was so upset by the woman's death that she climbed into her bunk and refused to get out. She soon found out that staying in bed was hard work, though. The *Georgiana* pitched and rolled so much that to avoid falling out of her bunk, Ann had to hook her feet under the bottom railings and brace herself with both arms.

burial

The ship was still thrashing from side to side when it became time for the baby's birth. Adoniram did all he could to make his wife comfortable, and after many hours of struggle, the baby was finally

Englishwoman = dead

born—dead. Adoniram buried his head in his arms and wept. He wept for himself, for Ann, for the little son they would never raise.

handwritten note: !! Son born DEAD

On deck things were not going well either. The *Georgiana* was difficult to handle, and she had been blown off course into the straits between the Little and Great Andaman Islands. As Adoniram walked wearily up on deck to get some fresh air, the captain greeted him. "If you are a praying man, now is the time to do it," he said in his Portuguese-accented English.

"Why is that?" asked Adoniram, wondering what could possibly go wrong now.

handwritten note: !! they've entered the worst strait in the ocean = certain death

"Look down there," the captain said, pointing to a pile of jagged black rocks jutting menacingly out of the water. "It's the worst reef in the Indian Ocean. I've never navigated this strait. No captain in his right mind would, but fate has left us no choice. The wind brought us here, and it's impossible to turn back."

"Couldn't we put in to shore and get some kind of pilot?" asked Adoniram, noting that both shorelines were very close.

"God forbid that should happen," replied the captain. "The natives in the Andamans don't take too kindly to strangers in their waters. If we put ashore or are shipwrecked, we'll be eaten for sure."

handwritten note: if they go to shore = eaten by Andamans

Adoniram gulped. "I'll pray," he said. "You can count on it."

Twenty minutes later Adoniram was back below deck with Ann, who was weak but recovering. "The ship is still," she said. "Thank God."

Adoniram held his wife's hand, unwilling to tell her that the quiet waters were caused by the shelter of the Andaman Islands and that the islands harbored natives who would gladly eat them if given the chance. Ann never knew the danger she was in as the captain skillfully maneuvered the *Georgiana* through the strait and back out into the open sea.

Three weeks after leaving Madras, Adoniram began to notice that the water sloshing around the ship was beginning to turn a muddy color. This could mean only one thing: They were near the delta of the Irrawaddy River. The next day, July 13, 1813, the *Georgiana* dropped anchor in the mouth of the Rangoon River, a channel of the Irrawaddy that ran across the delta to the sea. The river mouth was nearly a mile wide and was flanked by low banks thick with swamp grass.

They laid at anchor until a pilot came onboard to guide them upriver. As they began to move upstream, Adoniram stood on deck and stared at the country he had been planning for three years to make his home. They passed many small fishing villages with rickety houses built on stilts above the water. As he looked upriver, Adoniram could see something glistening in the afternoon sun over the top of the trees. If he had not read about the Shwe Dagon pagoda in Michael Symes's book *An Account of an Embassy to the Kingdom of Ava*, he would have been puzzled as to what he was seeing. However, from Symes's book he had learned it was the tallest of ten pagodas that had taken centuries to build. The pagoda stood over four hundred feet tall and was covered in pure gold. Inside were housed some of the most sacred Buddhist relics. Thousands of pilgrims came to pay homage to the Buddha each spring, and every three years a new layer of gold was hammered over the existing one.

As the ship got closer to Rangoon, Adoniram discovered that the city was not nearly as grand as the Shwe Dagon pagoda, nor was it at all like Calcutta. Rangoon was nothing more than a hugely overgrown village. There seemed to be few permanent buildings, the streets were muddy tracks, and the people were dressed like poor peasants.

When the *Georgiana* finally anchored off Rangoon, Adoniram went ashore for an hour before nightfall. Everything he saw confirmed his first impressions. Rangoon was a squalid city, more primitive and superstitious than any he had ever seen. His heart sank as he tried to describe it to his bedridden wife. Ann, who was normally cheerful, could take no more. She wept bitterly into her pillow. Unsure of what to do next, the Judsons prayed together. It was not the prayer of strong and courageous missionaries, however. Rather, it was the prayer of two grieving, desperately homesick and deeply discouraged people. "God," they prayed together, "we commend ourselves to You and ask that You would soon take us to heaven, where the wicked cease from troubling and the weary are at rest."

Chapter 10

Rangoon

The following morning there was nothing else Adoniram and Ann could do but disembark. Ann was too sick to walk, and an armchair with bamboo poles threaded through the arms was rigged to carry her. Adoniram walked along the deeply rutted road beside her. His wife was pale and scarcely moving. A large sunbonnet flopped down over her face. Adoniram anxiously hoped that now that she was back on solid ground she would soon recover. The hired servants carrying Ann set her down outside the customs house.

Within minutes, a crowd had gathered. Small children, completely naked, and many smoking cigars, giggled as they poked at Ann's shoes. Several older women, brightly dressed in long tunics, their well-oiled hair knotted back in tight buns, drew closer and closer.

"I bet they've never seen a white woman before," commented the captain of the *Georgiana* as he emerged from the customs house. "There's no one more inquisitive than a Burmese woman," he added. As if to confirm his words, one of the women dashed forward and pushed Ann's sunbonnet back out of the way so they could all see her face. A gasp went up from the crowd.

"See what I mean?" said the captain.

Ann smiled at the crowd, who giggled back.

"Go on in," continued the captain. "I've filled out your debarkation papers."

Adoniram motioned to the chair carriers who lifted Ann up again and carried her into the customs house. "House" was a rather grand name for the structure, which was really nothing more than a bamboo hut with woven grass sides. Through a series of gestures, Adoniram learned that one tenth of everything he had brought with him would be kept as a tax for the king. Both he and Ann were thoroughly searched to make sure they were not smuggling anything into Burma, and the correct papers were then stamped, and the couple was dismissed.

But where would they go? Adoniram knew of only one person in all of Burma, and that was William Carey's son Felix, who lived somewhere in Rangoon. As it turned out, the Careys' house was not far from the customs house. Soon Adoniram and Ann found themselves looking up at a stately

teak home, quite out of place because of its solid
construction. Adoniram pulled a rope attached to
a bell, and within a few seconds an old native man
appeared. The man was startled to see two white
people at the gate, and he immediately swung the
gate open and ushered the couple into a courtyard.
Soon a tall, slim woman arrived, trailed by three
toddlers. She was dark-skinned, but not as dark as
the Burmese people. Adoniram guessed she was
Felix Carey's wife, whom he had been told was part
Portuguese and part Burmese.

Carey's wife - Portu./Burm.

"Mrs. Carey?" he asked.

The woman nodded and lowered her eyes. "Yes.
My husband has gone to Ava," she said in broken
English. Then looking at Ann, she gestured, "Come
in, come in."

Over a lunch of tea and rice, Adoniram was able
to explain a little about who they were and why
they had come to Burma. Mrs. Carey listened atten-
tively and then invited the Judsons to stay with her
until Felix returned. With great relief, Adoniram left
Ann to rest and returned to the *Georgiana* to retrieve
their belongings and clear them through customs.
It took the rest of the day to accomplish this task,
but by nightfall everything the Judsons owned was
ashore. For better or for worse, they were now in
Burma.

got things & clear thru customs officially

Felix Carey arrived home the following day.
He explained that he had been in the royal city of
Ava vaccinating the young princes and princesses
against smallpox. Adoniram was intrigued by this.

in Burma

Ava = royal city (princesses & princes)
Carey = doctor

He had read about this modern idea of vaccination, but it was still very new and quite dangerous according to most people.

"I have studied it," Felix Carey said authoritatively, "and I am convinced it is the best way to stop this terrible scourge. The king has given me permission to vaccinate the entire province."

"Very impressive," replied Adoniram. "The king must trust you greatly."

Felix shrugged. "Today, perhaps, but tomorrow, who can say? Tomorrow he might decide to have my head. You can never tell in Burma."

Adoniram nodded. "So I hear," he said dryly.

Felix Carey continued. "It seems Providence has brought you here. My family and I are about to leave for a visit with my father in Serampore. My only worry in going was leaving this house with no Christian witness in it and not being able to continue work on my Burmese grammar book and Bible translation. But it seems God has it all under control. Your timing is perfect."

Adoniram gulped. "But," he spluttered, "how soon are you leaving?"

"Next week," replied Felix. "But don't worry, I will leave a housekeeper and a yard boy for you, and I know of a very good Burmese scholar who might be willing to teach you the language."

"Thank you," replied Adoniram, trying to digest the turn of events.

Over the next few days Adoniram and Felix Carey spent much time together. There were some customs Adoniram had to learn quickly, because to go against them could be fatal. Felix advised him to be very careful with his feet. "Know where they are pointed at all times," he warned.

"What do you mean?" asked Adoniram.

"The Burmese are very concerned about feet. Never touch anyone with your foot. Never point at anyone with your foot. Never sit so that the bottom of your feet are showing, and never ever stamp your feet. That's the most insulting thing you could ever do. You would never be forgiven for doing that."

Such talk made Adoniram feel very uneasy. He wondered what other mistakes he might make. Everything was so different, he could end up insulting the whole city and never even know it!

Two weeks later Adoniram and Ann were on their own. There was not another English-speaking person in all of Rangoon. The couple had to rely on Felix Carey's old servants to continue cooking and going about their business without any instructions from them.

Both Adoniram and Ann realized that learning the Burmese language was the most important thing they could do right then, and they began lessons immediately. The old scholar Felix Carey had recommended to teach them was a Hindu man who spoke no English. Lessons, which lasted for twelve hours a day, six days a week, were very frustrating at first. Adoniram and Ann had no way of discussing grammar or the makeup of the Burmese language with their teacher. Instead, they had to learn the language the way a little child would, by pointing at a familiar object and waiting to be told what its name was in Burmese.

Writing the language came a little easier, though. The Burmese alphabet consisted of many shapes made up of circles and arcs. It was not as difficult to write as it looked, and soon both Adoniram and Ann were filling pages with the rounded shapes that made up the language. However, when they came to writing words and sentences, they got a surprise. Written Burmese contained no periods, no commas, no question marks, no other punctuation marks of any kind. It did not even use spaces between the words. Since words all ran together, the reader had to make up his or her own mind where one word ended and another began. Thankfully Felix Carey had left the Judsons with the unfinished Burmese grammar book he was writing, and Adoniram and Ann were able to get some help from it as they studied. Adoniram loved the challenge of figuring the language out. It reminded him of the puzzle books his father had given him as a child.

The days turned into months as Adoniram and Ann struggled on learning Burmese. They were very lonely during this time, as only a handful of Europeans were in Rangoon, and they were either Portuguese or French. The couple longed for the opportunity to begin their missionary work proper, but both of them knew it was impossible without knowing the language.

Finally, in October 1813, three months after arriving in Burma, Adoniram decided it was time to visitging it up. "Oh Adoniram, I wish you had been there."

Adoniram grinned at her. His wife was always at her best in a crowd; he had known that since the day he met her back in New England. "Tell me all about it," he said.

"Well," started Ann, sinking into a wicker chair, "we arrived early, and the vicereine was taking a nap, so about ten of the viceroy's other wives entertained us. Actually, I think we entertained them. You should have seen them. They called their children, about twenty of them, and they all examined our clothes. They wanted to try on our bonnets and gloves and see our petticoats and stockings. I was just showing them what I kept in my pocket bag when the vicereine came in. You should have seen her, Adoniram. She is a beautiful woman, and she was wearing a gold embroidered gown and smoking a long, silver pipe."

Before continuing, Ann took a long sip from the cup of water the cook had brought for her. "When the vicereine walked into the room, all the other wives jumped out of the way and crouched down alongside the walls. The children all disappeared, too. The vicereine then beckoned Madame Duvall and me to sit on a mat with her. She asked so many questions. Sometimes I didn't know enough Burmese to answer them. I do hope she understood me."

"What kind of questions did she ask?" inquired

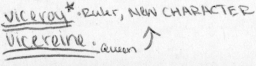

Adoniram.

"All sorts. How long do we intend to stay in Rangoon? Where did we come from? And how many wives you brought with you to Burma?!"

Adoniram chuckled at the vicereine's last question and then asked, "Did you get to see the viceroy?"

Ann nodded. "We had been talking for about half an hour when a servant announced his arrival. I got to my feet and bowed low, and when I looked up, there he was. What a fierce-looking man! He looked as though he had come straight from the battlefield. He was holding a six-foot-long spear and looked like he would order us out at any moment. But when he saw his wife, his demeanor softened, and he had a servant offer us drinks. He did not stay long, but I'm sure he knew I was your wife. When Madame Duvall and I were ready to leave, the vicereine grabbed my hand. She told me I must come back and visit her often and that she would consider me like a sister from now on."

Adoniram chuckled again. "You certainly make a better diplomat than I do," he said with admiration. "God willing, we will not need to call on the vicereine for special favors, but in Rangoon anything can happen."

In January 1814, Adoniram and Ann got to see for themselves just how cruel Burmese justice could be. The house next door was attacked by a band of about twenty robbers armed with swords and knives. The robbers stole everything they could carry and stabbed the owner to death as they left. A week later, seven of the thieves were found, and the viceroy decided to make an example of them. He ordered them to be displayed in the marketplace. Their hands and feet were tied, and their abdomens were cut open so their intestines spilled out. The robbers died a slow and painful death, and their bodies were left in the marketplace for three days for the local people to look at as a reminder of who was in control in Rangoon.

The sight of the three bodies sickened Adoniram and Ann, who worked even harder on their language studies. The need to share the gospel with the Burmese people and tell them about a new way to treat one another was more urgent than ever.

Around the middle of 1814, Felix Carey, his wife, and their three children arrived back in Rangoon. Felix had been offered a permanent post in the Royal government in Ava, and he had accepted the position. However, since this meant he would have to give up his missionary career, Adoniram and Ann would be the only "official" missionaries in Burma.

Adoniram and Ann liked Felix Carey and his family and had looked forward to getting to know them all better, so it was with mixed emotions that they said farewell to the Careys as they boarded a government boat for the journey upriver to Ava. It would have been an even sadder farewell had they known what lay ahead. Felix Carey was the only member of his family to survive the trip. The boat had sailed only a few miles upriver when a storm swept in, whipping up the surface of the river and capsizing the boat. Despite Felix's desperate attempts to save his family, his wife and three children were all drowned. Felix Carey himself was so traumatized by the event that he did not go on to Ava. Instead, he wandered off aimlessly into the Burmese interior.

Because of the poor communications in Burma, it was two weeks before Adoniram and Ann received word of the tragedy. They were both deeply saddened by the news.

Waiting two weeks before hearing news of the tragedy was nothing, though, compared to the length of time Adoniram and Ann had to wait for mail from the United States to arrive. It was three years and seven months after they sailed from Massachusetts before they got their first letter from America. The letter contained good news. Luther Rice had stayed true to his word. He had traveled up and down the East Coast of the United States stirring up interest in the establishment of a Baptist missionary society. In May 1814, such a society had been founded under the long name of the General Missionary Convention of the Baptist Denomination in the United States of America for Foreign Missions. Adoniram and Ann Judson had been appointed as the new society's first missionaries. Luther Rice was also being supported so that he could continue with the task of raising interest in and money for the new society.

Adoniram and Ann could not have been more pleased. Now they could write to William Carey and the English Baptist missionaries in Serampore and tell them they no longer needed their support.

As exciting as word of their new support was the news that another missionary couple, George and Phebe Hough, were on their way to join the Judsons in Burma. George was a printer by trade and was bringing a small printing press with him. This was more than Adoniram and Ann could have hoped for. They would no longer be the only missionaries in Burma.

All this good news, coupled with the fact that Ann was due to have a baby any day, lifted their spirits. On September 11, 1814, Adoniram delivered a healthy baby boy. He and Ann named their son Roger Williams Judson, after Roger Williams, an early missionary to the Indians in New England. Both Ann and Adoniram hoped that their son, like his namesake, would grow up to be a missionary.

Roger Williams Judson was the first white baby to be born in Rangoon, and whenever Ann took him out of the house, a crowd gathered. "Look how white his feet are!" they would exclaim, or, "His eyes are the color of the sky!"

By now the Judsons' hard work was beginning to pay off. Ann was able to speak fluent Burmese, while Adoniram, who had spent hundreds of hours with his tutor, had a deep understanding of how the language was put together and had nearly finished writing the Burmese grammar book Felix Carey had begun. It looked as though the hard times were behind them. The viceroy accepted their presence, *every-thing going great*

more missionaries were on their way, Adoniram and Ann were healthy, the baby was thriving, and the missionaries were beginning to have meaningful conversations with the local people about the gospel. It seemed nothing could go wrong now.

Losses and Gains

Roger Judson turned six months old in March 1816. It was about this time that his parents noticed something strange. During the day Roger was fine. He would lie on his mat in Adoniram's study following his father's every move, or he would crawl around the garden. He enjoyed all the attention he got on outings with his parents around Rangoon. At night, however, he was a different child. His face felt feverish, and he cried and fussed for hours. Adoniram and Ann worried over what the problem could be. Neither of them knew enough about babies to decide whether it was normal teething behavior or if their son had something more serious wrong with him. Only time would tell, and it did.

!!
Roger
died!

Exactly two weeks after Adoniram and Ann first noticed Roger's high temperature at night, the baby had a coughing fit. Nothing his frantic parents did for him seemed to help. Within an hour, Roger was dead.

"little white child"

The grief over Roger's death sent Adoniram and Ann into deep depression. Ann wanted to know if all their children were going to be taken from them. Adoniram had no answer for her as he dug a small grave for his son under the mango tree in the mission house garden. News spread quickly of Roger's death, and later that day, over two hundred friends and acquaintances arrived in time for the funeral of the "little white child."

CC
Depressed

For the next three days, neither Adoniram nor Ann had the heart to go out in public. Instead, they locked themselves away in the mission house, surrounded by the few physical reminders of their dead son; a crib, the tiny clothes he wore, and his mat on the floor.

!!
vicereine
visits

On the fourth day, Ann looked out the window and let out a surprised gasp. "Adoniram," she called, "the vicereine is on her elephant, and she is stopped outside the gate."

22

why with guards

TQ

Adoniram hurried to the window. His mouth fell open as he counted the number of officers and attendants the vicereine had with her. There were over two hundred of them. "What can this mean?" he asked anxiously, slipping on his jacket.

"I'm not sure," replied Ann. "I have not been to visit her lately. I hope she's not offended."

The Judsons stood transfixed as the vicereine, dressed in a blue and gold silk robe, was lifted down from the elephant and set on the ground.

"Come on," said Adoniram, grabbing Ann's hand. "We had better welcome her."

When they opened the gate, the vicereine stepped into the courtyard.

"My dear sister," she began, holding out her hands to Ann. "I have only just heard of your son's death. Why did you not send for me so I could come to the funeral?"

Adoniram watched his wife turn white and supposed she, too, was thinking of the penalty a person could pay for offending a member of the viceroy's family.

Ann quickly regained her composure. "I am sorry," she replied. "I was so shocked by Roger's death that I did not think of it."

"Ah, well, I am here now," replied the vicereine, patting Ann on the hand. "It is not good to shut yourself away like this. Tomorrow I will send an elephant for you both, and you shall be my guests for an outing."

Neither Adoniram nor Ann felt like going on an outing, but deep down they both knew they had to find a way to put their baby son's death behind them and go on.

Sure enough, the following morning a huge elephant arrived outside the mission house, complete with a howdah, a little booth perched on the animal's back in which Adoniram and Ann were to sit. A rope ladder was dropped, and the two of them were helped up onto the elephant's back. The driver, who sat just behind the elephant's ears, skillfully guided the animal down the road to the corner, where the vicereine was waiting on her own elephant. Looking very regal in her gold-covered howdah, the vicereine smiled and waved to Adoniram and Ann.

Soon the procession of elephants and people had walked through town and out into the jungle around Rangoon. Despite their recent loss, Adoniram and Ann were fascinated by the whole adventure. Their elephant walked side-by-side with the vicereine's. In front of them were thirty men with guns and spears, each man clad in a red tunic and wearing a long, floppy hat that reached to his shoulders. Behind them were four more elephants carrying the viceroy's son and important government officials. And behind them was a throng of nearly three hundred servants carrying everything from huge fans to a supply of the vicereine's favorite cigars.

From his position on the elephant's back, Adoniram was able to get a sense of the animal's strength. As they ventured deeper into the jungle, the path became narrower. At one point, the driver tapped the elephant with a stick, and the huge animal stopped and wound its trunk around the tree in front of it. The howdah swayed as the great beast braced its back legs and pulled the tree out of the ground by its roots. The elephant tossed the tree to one side and lumbered on down the path.

sitting

Finally, the procession reached an open spot under a huge banyan tree, where the vicereine signaled the procession to stop. "This will be a fine place for our meal," she said, smiling at Ann.

Ann nodded and waited to be helped down the fifteen feet from the elephant's back to the ground, where they all ate an enjoyable lunch. The vicereine did everything she could to take Adoniram's and Ann's minds off their dead son.

The vicereine's efforts seemed to pay off, and soon both of the Judsons began to focus again on their missionary work. Ann, who was very lonely without Roger, decided to throw herself into starting a school to teach girls how to read. Most of the boys in Burma learned to read, but not the girls, and Ann wanted to do something about it. Soon there were twenty, then thirty girls lined up at the mission house each morning waiting for Ann to begin reading lessons. After class, when the mothers came to collect their daughters, Ann would tell Bible stories. Many of the women would stay for twenty minutes or longer to listen to the strange tales the white woman told them fluently in their own language.

Ann did reading lessons.

In October, the Houghs and their printing press finally arrived in Rangoon, along with a supply of paper and Burmese type faces, generously made up for them by the head printer in Serampore. The first thing to be done after their arrival was to build a small hut for the printing press. Then it was time for George Hough to learn as much as possible about the Burmese language so that he could set the type.

Oct - Hughs arrived

AA
Smart
Busy

While helping to set up the printing press, Adoniram kept busy translating the book of Matthew into Burmese. He also held nightly meetings with local Burmese men. Ann was busy, too. Her school for girls was flourishing, and she also had set about assisting Adoniram with the task of writing some simple Christian literature to help the Burmese people understand about God. This task was much more difficult than it may have sounded to their Baptist supporters back in New England.

Buddhist
religion
=
reincarnation
until
you
reach
Nirvana

Most Burmese people were Buddhist and did not believe in an eternal God. They had no concept of such a being. For them, human life was an endless wheel of reincarnation, of being born and reborn from one life to the next. This cycle was marked by endless suffering caused by a person's passions and selfish desire for things that could not satisfy the spirit. The only hope of salvation for these Buddhists was to follow the Noble Eightfold Path laid out by the Buddha more than two and a half thousand years before. A person who disciplined himself and followed this path could eventually reach Nirvana—the state of no longer being alive—and so be freed from the cycle of being born and reborn. It was a bleak outlook, completely at odds with the hope and promise of salvation from sin and a new life here and now and in heaven to come, held out by Christianity, which Adoniram and Ann were trying to share with the Burmese people.

It took a while, but finally Adoniram and Ann produced a seven-page tract that they felt explained

Produced a tract & printed it

the gospel in a way that Burmese people could understand. They concluded the tract by noting the date it was completed, according to both the English and the Burmese calendars: "In the year of Christ, 1816; in the Burman year 1178; in the 967th day of the lord of the Saddan elephant, and the master of the Sakyah weapon; and in the 33rd year of his reign; in the division Pashoo; on Tuesday, the 12th day of the wane of the moon Wahgoung, after the double beat, this writing, entitled *The Way to Heaven*, was finished. May the reader obtain light. Amen."

The type was set for the tract, and in early 1817, a thousand copies were printed by George Hough. At first no one seemed very interested in reading the tract, but slowly word got around that the foreigners had a "holy book," and men began to stop by the mission house and request a copy of it. Sometimes they would stay and ask questions, but most often they just took the tract and quickly left. It was surprising, then, to Adoniram when one day in March 1817 he answered the door to find a man who wished to come inside and talk.

"My name is Maung Yah," the man said. "I have come to visit you."

"Please sit down," replied Adoniram, taking note of the man's expensive clothing. "Where are you from?"

"North of here," replied the man rather vaguely. "I have come to Rangoon to worship at the Shwe Dagon pagoda."

Adoniram nodded. In Burma, March was Tabaung, the last month of the Burmese year and the month in which huge Buddhist festivals were held. Tens of thousands of pilgrims from all over Burma flocked to Rangoon to worship at the pagoda where eight hairs of the great Buddha were said to be enshrined.

Maung Yah leaned towards Adoniram, his voice low and steady, his dark eyes gleaming. "How long will it take me to learn the religion of Jesus?" he asked.

Adoniram stared for a moment. In his four years in Rangoon he had never been asked this question. Could it be that this man wanted to become a Christian? "Well," he began, stumbling over his words, "it's impossible to answer that question. It depends on how serious a person is in his inquiry. If a man or a woman sincerely wishes to become a Christian, God will give them light. If a person does not sincerely wish to become a Christian, they will never truly understand the Christian message."

"It is more complicated than I had imagined," replied Maung Yah.

"God is there to help anyone who asks," said Adoniram gently. "Tell me, how did you come to hear of Jesus?"

Maung Yah's face brightened. "He is the Son of God," he said. "And God is a being without beginning or end, who is not subject to old age or death, but always is."

A chill went up and down Adoniram's spine. Those were the exact words of the tract he and Ann had written. Sitting cross-legged in front of him was proof that the printed word could make a difference with the Burmese people. Maung Yah was the first Burmese person Adoniram had ever heard speak directly of an eternal being.

"Wait here," said Adoniram, hurrying over to his desk to retrieve a copy of a new tract Ann had just finished writing. "I see you are familiar with my writing," he said.

Maung Yah nodded as he took the tract. "Yes," he said. "These words speak of the right way. This is the true God."

Thinking that the man was ready to become a Christian, Adoniram began to tell him more about Christianity, but Maung Yah did not want to talk anymore.

"I need more of the writings," he told Adoniram several times. "What can you give me to read and meditate on?"

Adoniram felt deflated. He had not yet finished translating the book of Matthew. He explained to Maung Yah that if he came back at this time next year he would have a big book for him with the entire life of the Son of God recorded in it. But Maung Yah was not to be satisfied. "You must have something," he said.

In the end, Adoniram handed him the proof sheets George Hough had printed of the first five chapters of Matthew. Although they had many mistakes in them, Maung Yah seemed happy to have the pages.

"I will read them every day," he promised Adoniram. "I will guard them as a great treasure."

For weeks Adoniram waited for news from Maung Yah. Surely he must have become a Christian by now, he told himself. Still no news came. In frustration, Adoniram talked to his language teacher about the difficulty the mission was having in making a single convert.

The teacher's answer was simple and to the point. "We are from Burma, the Golden Country," he said. "Everyone who is from Burma is a Buddhist, and just a few are Hindu like myself. That is the way it is. Your religion might be good for foreigners, but not for us; we are from Burma. Look around. Do you see even a single native Christian in all of Burma? No. Even if your religion was truer than ours, our people would rather dwell in hell with their families than in heaven alone."

Adoniram sighed deeply at the response. But it was true. During the past year, hundreds of people had taken a tract or come to listen to him or Ann talk, but not one of them had become a convert. There had to be a key to unlock their hearts, but Adoniram had no idea what it might be. Somehow he had to find a way to convince Burmese people that they could become Christians and still be Burmese.

Chapter 12

The Voyage to Nowhere

It was December 1, 1817, and Adoniram was halfway through his early morning walk around Rangoon when he stopped dead in the middle of a muddy street. "Why didn't I think of it before," he laughed out loud to himself. "Of course. That's the answer."

Adoniram hurried home to Ann, the idea percolating in his head as he walked. "Ann, I have the answer!" he called as he walked into the courtyard of the mission house.

"To what?" Ann called back from the other end of the house.

"To the problem of being Burmese and being a Christian."

131

Ann walked into the courtyard and gave her husband her full attention.

"Remember the letter we received last week from William Carey?" asked Adoniram.

Ann nodded.

"In the letter Carey said there is a handful of Burmese Christians living in Chittagong. Well, I've been thinking. What if I were to go to Chittagong and invite one or two of these Christians to join us in Rangoon. They could preach and answer questions. Surely then the people here couldn't argue that it's impossible to be Burmese and a Christian. We would have a Burmese Christian to introduce to them and prove them wrong."

Adoniram watched as his wife's eyes shone. "It's a wonderful idea," Ann said. "Just what the Burmese people need to see. And now's a perfect time to go to Chittagong. The Houghs are here to help run the mission. And a sea voyage is just what you need to give your eyes a rest," she added.

"Yes," said Adoniram. "It won't be easy, though, finding a ship going that way, but I'll start looking."

Adoniram began keeping a close eye on ships coming and going from Rangoon, hoping to find one headed for Chittagong, a small seaport at the northern end of the Bay of Bengal, about two hundred miles east of Calcutta and fifty miles west of Burma's border with India. Since Chittagong was so close to Burma, many Burmese people from the neighboring province of Arakan lived there. A Dutch missionary had also taken up residence there and was busy sharing the gospel with these Burmese people.

With favorable winds, it normally took about two weeks by ship to get to Chittagong from Rangoon. Adoniram hoped to find a ship headed northwest to Calcutta that would make a detour and stop in at Chittagong so that he could disembark. Once he had convinced one or two of the Burmese Christians there to return with him, he would search for a ship that could bring them all back to Rangoon.

After a week of looking, Adoniram could hardly believe it when the *Two Brothers* sailed into Rangoon. The *Two Brothers* was apparently about to make a round trip to Chittagong, something he had never heard of a ship doing from Rangoon before. Surely, he told Ann, this was God's way of telling him now was the right time to go.

On Christmas Day 1817, the *Two Brothers* hoisted sail and headed off down the Rangoon River bound for Chittagong. Almost immediately Adoniram became violently ill. He thought it was a combination of seasickness and the intense headaches he had been experiencing as a result of eyestrain. The captain assured him that they would be in Chittagong in ten or twelve days, and Adoniram reassured himself that he could easily endure any discomfort for that length of time.

By the end of the second day, the *Two Brothers* was being lashed by strong headwinds. The captain visited Adoniram, his sole passenger, and explained that the voyage might take a day or two longer than first thought because of the adverse winds. He was wrong. The *Two Brothers* was buffeted by the wind and pummeled by the seething ocean for an entire month, first in the Gulf of Martaban off Burma and then out in the Bay of Bengal. By the end of January, Adoniram was convinced that the captain had no idea how to manage his ship or his crew. At the rate they were proceeding, it would take them three more months to reach Chittagong, and they were already running dangerously short of food and fresh water.

On February 1, 1818, long past the date Adoniram had anticipated being in Chittagong, the captain finally decided it was hopeless trying to reach their original destination. He gave the order for the crew to turn the ship southwest and follow the prevailing winds to Madras, India.

The whole turn of events reminded Adoniram very much of when he had been kidnapped by privateers in the Atlantic Ocean. Once again he was half-starved and headed to somewhere he did not want to go.

With the wind at her back, the *Two Brothers* made good time crossing the Bay of Bengal. But as the ship approached the coast of India, the winds shifted and conspired with the tides to beat her back. The captain spent another month trying unsuccessfully to maneuver the ship close enough to land to drop anchor off Madras. By now it was the end of February, and the situation onboard was desperate. There was no food or water left on the ship, and the only way to get any was to beg it from the few native boats that ventured out that far into the Indian Ocean. On a good day, each person aboard the *Two Brothers* was lucky to get a cup of water and a spoonful of moldy rice.

For Adoniram, things were even more desperate. What at first had seemed like a case of seasickness had turned into dysentery. Adoniram was too sick to eat, and his raging fever could not be quenched by the small amount of water he was given each day. He lay in his bunk for days on end, too weak to get up. He only faintly understood when the captain came to tell him he had abandoned all hope of reaching Madras and instead the ship was now headed three hundred miles farther north to the small port of Masulipitam.

Adoniram began to fade in and out of consciousness. When he was conscious, he thought about Ann back in Rangoon. He wondered how long it would be after his death before she received word of it. Finally, three months to the day after setting out so optimistically from Rangoon, the *Two Brothers* arrived off the coast of Masulipitam. The sea was now calm, and the crew were eager to go ashore. The captain asked Adoniram if he would like to be carried ashore, but Adoniram could hardly concentrate long enough to think about what to do next. Eventually, though, he managed to scribble a note. He addressed it to "Any English Resident" and begged whoever read the note to come and get him from the ship so that he could die in peace on dry land.

Late in the afternoon, a boat rowed by British soldiers in red uniforms came to collect Adoniram. The soldiers lifted him onto their boat, where he lay drooped across the bow as they rowed him ashore. Adoniram was met at the dock by a British army officer, who insisted Adoniram be his personal guest.

With some fresh clothes to wear, a cool bed to lie upon and plenty of food and water, Adoniram made a speedy recovery, which astonished him. He had been certain he was going to die. But instead of being laid out in a coffin, he was up and strolling around. Once his strength returned, Adoniram turned his attention to getting back to Rangoon. He fretted that Ann, after not hearing a word from him in nearly four months, would imagine the worst, and he was eager to get back to her. However, he flatly refused to reboard the *Two Brothers*, and sail south to Madras, the nearest major Indian port, where there was usually a steady stream of ships coming and going. Instead, he decided to travel the three hundred miles to Madras overland.

On April 1, 1818, Adoniram thanked the British officer for his kindness and generosity and set out to hire a palanquin, a padded box carried by four men. As he traveled along in the palanquin towards Madras, Adoniram thought about how things had changed in India for him. Where once he had been hounded by British officials who wanted to arrest him and deport him to England, now a British army officer had taken him in and shown him great kindness. He had done so not only because Adoniram was in such obvious need but also because the East India Company was now a little more tolerant of missionaries coming to India, though it still exercised great power over who was and wasn't allowed to stay in the country. As well, it was obvious to all, even the most narrow-minded East India Company official, that Adoniram had not come to India to stay as a missionary, rather he was the innocent victim of regrettable circumstances that had marooned him in the country. As soon as he could, he would be on his way back to Burma.

When Adoniram finally reached Madras, more disappointment awaited him. Not a single ship in the harbor was headed north farther on up the Bay of Bengal, and none was expected until July or August. Once again, Adoniram felt trapped. He could do nothing but wait and pray that he would make it back to Rangoon soon.

In Madras, the Reverend Mr. Thomason, a chaplain with the East India Company, invited Adoniram to stay with him for as long as he needed. Appreciative of the offer, Adoniram tried to make himself useful, helping Mr. Thomason wherever and however he could. At lunchtime each day, he walked to the docks to see whether any new ships were on the horizon.

In late July, Adoniram finally found a captain whose ship was headed for Rangoon. But before he booked passage, he made some inquiries about the ship and its captain. He had no intention of being buffeted around the Bay of Bengal for another three months at the hands of an incompetent mariner. Everything was in order, and so with great relief Adoniram said farewell to Mr. Thomason and set sail for Rangoon.

Thankfully, the trip back was swift and comfortable. On August 2, 1818, Adoniram stood on deck and watched happily as the pilot boat slipped through the mouth of the Rangoon River on its way to meet them. His happiness was short-lived though. The pilot had some disturbing news for Adoniram. As far as he was aware, the mission in Rangoon had broken up. Adoniram questioned him repeatedly, but it was no use. The pilot did not know anything more, and he had no idea what had happened to the missionaries.

The trip up the Rangoon River seemed agonizingly slow to Adoniram as he fretted about whether Ann was dead or alive. And he wondered why the mission had broken up. And what had happened to the printing press and his nearly completed revision of the Burmese grammar book and dictionary? The questions plagued him, but he knew there would be no answers until he reached Rangoon.

Long afternoon shadows stretched across the countryside when the golden roof of the Shwe Dagon pagoda came into view, looming above the jungle. Adoniram was nearly home. He went below and collected his things. He didn't have much, since he had packed only enough for about a month, not for the seven months it had been since he set sail from Rangoon. And while he was disappointed to be returning without a single Burmese Christian, the thought paled in comparison to the fears he had for his wife's safety.

Tears of joy welled up in Adoniram's eyes and streamed down his face when he saw Ann standing next to George Hough on the dock. His wife was alive and well! Adoniram rushed down the gangplank as soon as it was lowered, and he embraced Ann. Together they talked long into the night. Ann insisted Adoniram tell her his story first. She wanted to know where he had been and why he hadn't brought any Burmese Christians back with him from Chittagong.

When Adoniram was done telling her of all his misadventures, Ann told him of all that had happened in Rangoon since he had left. He was shocked by the awful things that had occurred during his seven-month absence. Ann explained that for the first month all had gone well. The vicereine had come and taken her on several elephant expeditions. She had even asked Ann some searching questions about the Christian tracts she had seen. But after that, things changed fast. The viceroy was promoted, and he and the vicereine had moved to the royal city of Ava. The new viceroy of Rangoon was a single man, and so Ann, being a woman, could not present herself to him. Women in Burma were not permitted to speak to male officials. Regrettably, George Hough did not know much Burmese, so the missionaries had no proper way of introducing themselves to the new viceroy. Soon after the new viceroy's arrival, an order came from the courthouse for George Hough to present himself there. No reason was given why his presence was required, and Ann began to fear something bad was going to happen now that they were no longer under the favor of the viceroy.

George Hough went to the courthouse, where officials told him that all foreign teachers had been banned from Burma and if George did not tell the Burmese officials everything he had been doing in Rangoon, they would write their report with his blood. The officials arrested him and questioned him for two days. Since George could speak only few words of Burmese and the officials could not speak a word of English, the questioning was long and torturous.

"It was about then a ship from Chittagong brought news that you had not landed there," said Ann, sighing deeply. "I knew ships were often swept off course, but I did begin to worry."

Adoniram reached over and clasped his wife's hand. "I am sorry to have put you through that," he said. "But tell me, what happened next? Why did they let George Hough go?"

Ann smiled. "I was beginning to give up hope of ever seeing him or you again when our Burmese language teacher came to visit. He suggested I write a petition on behalf of the mission and submit it to the viceroy. In doing so, he told me, we would find out whether the viceroy had ordered George Hough's arrest or if his officials had done so without his knowledge in order to try to extract a bribe from the mission in return for George's release. The viceroy was very angry when he read the petition. 'Why has the foreign teacher been treated this way?' he demanded of his officials. The officials got the message, and after an apology from them, George Hough was released and wasn't bothered again. But no sooner had he been released than something much worse happened: Cholera broke out."

[handwritten margin notes: viceroy didn't ban the foreign teacher — servants bribed !! — Cholera broke out]

"How can that be?" interjected Adoniram. "Cholera is found only in India."

"Not anymore," replied his wife grimly. "There was no mistaking it. It was awful. Thousands of people died. The death drums beat all day and all night. It was so frightening. A healthy person could wake up well and happy in the morning and be in his grave by dinnertime. I was scared. Sometimes I wished you were here with me, and other times I was glad you were away from the terrible disease."

[handwritten margin notes: setting US — setting: Burmese vs British]

Adoniram could see Ann's eyes welling up with tears, which Ann dabbed with the corner of a handkerchief. "On top of that," she said after regaining her composure, "the ships that did come to Rangoon brought rumors of a war brewing between the Burmese and the British. Did you hear anything about it in Madras?"

Adoniram nodded. "I heard that tensions were building along the border between Burma and India."

"Fortunately the rumors didn't come to anything, but they scared Phebe Hough so much she insisted that George and she move to Calcutta," said Ann.

"And what made them change their minds?" asked Adoniram.

"They haven't," said Ann. "In fact, they left on a ship a week ago, but it had to turn back when it got to the open sea. The cargo in the hold shifted dangerously. As soon as it's reloaded, they intend to be off again. George packed up the printing press, and it's stowed onboard the ship."

Adoniram frowned. "But the press was donated for use in Burma," he said, a note of frustration and disappointment in his voice.

"I know," replied Ann soothingly. "George says he will keep printing anything we translate. He just wants to do it at a safe distance from Rangoon, that's all."

Adoniram and Ann sat in silence for a moment.

"Oh, I almost forgot!" exclaimed Ann. "There is one piece of good news. I received a letter two months ago saying the Baptist missions board is sending out two new missionaries and their wives to join us. They are the Wheelocks and the Colmans."

Adoniram smiled broadly. "God takes one family from us and replaces it with two," he chuckled. "Thank goodness Luther Rice went back to the United States to stir up interest in missionary work."

"Think what we'll be able to do with three missionary families here," said Ann excitedly. "I just know everything is going to work out fine, especially now that you're home."

As Adoniram Judson looked into his wife's bright blue eyes sparkling with hope, he almost convinced himself she was right. But deep down inside, he had a nagging feeling the worst was yet to come.

Into the Golden Presence

Six weeks later, in mid-September 1818, two young missionary men and their wives disembarked in Rangoon. Adoniram rushed to the dock to meet them. At first he was shocked at how young they were: Edward Wheelock was twenty-two, his wife, Eliza, was twenty, and James and Lucy Colman were both twenty-three. But then he realized he had been only twenty-four himself when he set out from New England to be a missionary. And like him, what they lacked in age they made up for in enthusiasm. They were adaptable, too. Back at the mission house, no one complained about the overcrowding or the new diet, which consisted of strange foods like curry and tropical vegetables that had never made their way to New England. Within

[handwritten margin notes: mid Sept. / missionaries arrive / NEW PPL]

145

[handwritten note: Edward Wheelock & Eliza (22 & 20) / James & Lucy (23 & 23)]

days, the four new missionaries were hard at work learning the Burmese language. They were helped greatly in this by the grammar book and dictionary Adoniram had written.

But the new missionaries' industrious start quickly came to a halt when James Colman and Edward Wheelock both became ill on the same day. The men coughed up blood and complained of chest pain. Adoniram was not a doctor, but he didn't have to be to know what was wrong. Both men had the classic signs of tuberculosis.

After many weeks of constant nursing, James Colman began to make a slow recovery, but Edward Wheelock continued to grow thinner and weaker. At the same time, something just as bad was happening to his wife. As Edward's body got sicker and sicker, so did Eliza's mind. Unable to accept that her husband was dying from tuberculosis, Eliza began imagining that the people in the mission house were using some secret means to slowly kill him. Eventually she decided that if her husband was to survive, they both needed to "escape" from Rangoon. Adoniram and Ann begged Eliza to change her mind, but she insisted on setting sail for India with her gravely ill husband. A week out to sea, in a raging storm, Edward Wheelock used his last ounce of strength to clamber up on deck, where he threw himself overboard and drowned. Adoniram never heard from Eliza again. James Colman did not meet the same fate. After hovering at death's door for many months, he made a full recovery.

As the mission house got back to "normal," Adoniram decided it was time to make a bold move. He and Ann had spent six years learning the Burmese language, telling Bible stories and translating Scripture, but they had not managed to find a place where the people felt comfortable enough to sit and talk one-on-one with them. Few Burmese people came to the mission house now that there was a new viceroy in Rangoon. The Judsons needed to find some sort of "neutral ground" where they could meet with the Burmese.

6 years in Burma

This neutral ground came in the form of a tract of land at the rear of the mission house that came up for sale. The front boundary of the land was on Pagoda Road, the main walking street in Rangoon. Adoniram purchased the land, and he and James Colman set about building a *zayat,* an open building with a roof but no sides, where Burmese people—especially people who were on pilgrimages—liked to gather to talk. Since there was always some pilgrimage or another to the Shwe Dagon pagoda at the end of Pagoda Road, thousands of people would pass the zayat each day.

setting for new building

maybe more Christian Reach

By the beginning of April 1819, the building was finished. It wasn't the biggest or the grandest zayat by any stretch of the imagination, but it was a start, a place where the missionaries could discuss religion and answer questions freely with the Burmese people.

Day after day, Adoniram would sit on the steps of the zayat and yell his invitation to passersby.

• Built a zayat 4 Bible discussions

"Ho! Everyone who thirsts for knowledge enter here." And people did come in. Some came to jeer and insult Adoniram, some to drink tea and rest. A few came to listen to the words of this new religion Christianity.

One of the very first men Adoniram noticed paying close attention to what he said was Maung Nau, a single man, about thirty-five years old. Maung Nau was poor and went from job to job. The first day he visited was a Friday. Since he sat quietly and never asked a question, Adoniram was surprised to see him return on Saturday, and then for a church service on Sunday, and again on Monday. Indeed, by Wednesday, May 5, Adoniram was able to make an entry in his journal that he had waited many years to write: "I am beginning to think that the Grace of God has reached his [Maung Nau's] heart.... It seems almost too much to believe that God has begun to manifest his grace on the Burmans; but this day I could not resist the delightful conviction that this is really the case."

Adoniram was not mistaken. Maung Nau wanted to learn more about Christianity, and by the following Sunday, he had made his decision to become a Christian. Much to Adoniram's delight, he showed his determination by standing up and announcing his conversion to his fellow countrymen at the zayat.

Not wanting to lose this wonderful opportunity, Adoniram invited Maung Nau to live at the mission house. In that way, the new convert could learn more about his new faith, as well as help to distribute Christian literature. The day Maung Nau moved in was one of the happiest days of Adoniram's life. Adoniram had tried to go to Chittagong and bring back a Burmese Christian to help share the gospel, but the attempt had failed miserably. Now he had a Burmese Christian from Rangoon to help him.

It was only a month before Maung Nau asked to be baptized. At first Adoniram was delighted by the request, but slowly a chill began to spread through his heart. It had nothing to do with Maung Nau. Quite the contrary, Maung Nau was a true convert in every sense of the word, daily studying, praying, even preaching. The feeling of dread Adoniram was experiencing had to do with events in Rangoon. Adoniram couldn't put his finger on it, but he knew something was wrong. Minor officials, who only a month before would have bowed to him in the street now harassed him. Almost every day, an official would appear at the door of the mission house demanding money in the form of a bribe or a tax. This was not normal, and Adoniram wondered what could have happened to embolden these minor officials. These changing circumstances made him reluctant to baptize the mission's very first Burmese convert until he understood what was happening in the country. He felt it was just too risky for all concerned to go ahead with the baptism.

While Adoniram was puzzling over the behavior of the government officials in Rangoon, the viceroy ordered a hundred boats be made ready to transport him upriver to Ava. It was the most lavish display of pomp and ceremony Adoniram and Ann had seen in Burma. It left Adoniram wondering more than ever about what was happening. And he was not the only one. The entire city was now seething with whispers and rumors.

Early on Thursday, the day after the viceroy's departure, Adoniram visited a number of zayats around Rangoon to see if he could learn the reason for the tension in the air. At about ten in the morning, as he sat in a zayat talking with some Burmese men, a man ran up. "There's to be a reading at the court," the man said, panting to a stop in front of the zayat.

Adoniram quickly left the zayat and began walking briskly across town to the court. He hoped he was finally going to get some answers. Soon a throng of people was gathered outside the court. When a royal messenger arrived, the crowd parted for him. The messenger, dressed in red, the color of the royal household, stood on a carved box and opened a scroll. He began to read: "Listen ye: The immortal king, wearied, it would seem, with the fatigues of royalty, has gone up to amuse himself in the celestial regions. His grandson, the heir apparent, is seated on the throne. The young monarch enjoins us all to remain quiet and to wait his imperial orders."

The messenger rolled up the scroll, and the crowd parted for him once again. As soon as he was out of earshot, the throng erupted with questions. How long had the king been dead? What changes would the new king make in his realm? What had happened to old King Bodawpaya's two sons, the new king's uncles?

In the midst of all the noise and confusion, Adoniram slipped through the crowd and made his way home. Ann and James and Lucy Colman would be waiting to hear the news.

As more news from the royal city of Ava slowly drifted into Rangoon, Adoniram began to understand why the local officials had been acting the way they had. It turned out that King Bodawpaya had died two weeks before the decree was read in Rangoon. The new king, Bagyidaw, following the tradition of countless Burmese rulers before him, had eliminated anyone who might have the slightest reason to be disloyal to him. All of the previous king's servants, as well as most of his army, were killed. The king also had his uncles, along with many provincial leaders, tortured and strangled. He even ordered that his brothers, nieces, and nephews be sewn into red sacks and thrown into the river to drown. (He used red sacks on account of their royal standing.)

The reign of terror lasted for ten days, and at the end of it, the dead were counted. Fourteen hundred members of the royal household and other officials, along with twelve thousand commoners, had been killed. After the killing was over, King Bagyidaw felt confident enough to send out messengers to the provinces to announce that he was now king. That was why the local officials had been so greedy lately, seeking out bribes and illegal taxes. These officials had been trying to gather as much wealth as possible for themselves while their superiors were busy trying to save their heads.

The new king sounded particularly harsh to Adoniram, who hoped it would be a long time before he ever had to meet him. However, circumstances soon made it necessary for him to visit the man who had just ordered the deaths of thousands of his subjects.

By November 1819, there were two more Burmese converts, Maung Thahlah and Maung Byaay (Maung is a title meaning "young man"). Both men asked to be baptized just as Maung Nau had done. On the one hand, the Judsons and the Colmans were excited to have three new Christians, who together brought the total number of Protestants in Burma to seven. (Some Burmese people with Portuguese parents or grandparents were Roman Catholics, though most of the people were active participants in Buddhist rituals.) On the other hand, the new Christian converts had created a lot of suspicion among people in Rangoon. Up until then, the missionaries had been looked upon with pity by the locals. Indeed, their goal of making converts seemed ridiculous. Everyone knew that a Burmese Buddhist would never renounce his or her faith and become a Christian. Christianity was for white people.

But now three men had converted, and things had changed. Suddenly the missionaries were a threat to the Buddhist way of life. As a result, the work of the mission came to a standstill. No one wanted to be seen within a hundred feet of Adoniram or his coworkers. The zayat remained empty day after day, and the officials found creative and petty ways to harass them. As well, the new king ordered many more Buddhist zayats to be built and staffed with priests. Adoniram and Ann and the Colmans felt as if a noose were being tightened around their necks. Something had to be done.

In a letter sent home to his family, Adoniram explained why he had decided to go to Ava to see the king about the situation: "Our business must be fairly laid before the king. If he frowns upon us, all missionary attempts within his dominion will be out of the question. If he favors us, none of our enemies, during the continuance of his favor, can touch a hair of our heads."

As Adoniram and James Colman left Rangoon for Ava, they did not know whether they would ever see their wives again. King Bagyidaw was ruthless and had no reason to allow the Christian religion to be preached in his kingdom. Not only that, the three-hundred-fifty-mile trip upriver to Ava was extremely dangerous.

The route to Ava took the men up the Rangoon River until it joined the Irrawaddy. Then the men followed the Irrawaddy River deep into the heart of Burma. Only a handful of Europeans had ever been to the Golden City, as Ava was known. As their boat moved farther upstream, Adoniram marveled

New Capital Not in Ava

at the number of abandoned cities that lay along the banks of the river. This occurred because of an unusual Burmese custom. For thousands of years, each newly crowned king had insisted on having a new capital city built in his honor. These were huge, lavish cities, each one supposedly more impressive than the previous king's. All royal and government business was transferred to the new city, while the old city was left to rot and be engulfed by the jungle. Indeed, King Bagyidaw had already established Amarapura as the new royal capital. Amarapura was a little south of Ava, the previous king's capital. However, most people continued to refer to the place as Ava, since Amarapura was actually more of an extension of the old royal city than a completely new city on its own.

New capital

A few people still lived among the old abandoned government buildings, temples, and pagodas that lined the river, but they were mostly outcasts or the dreaded "dacoits." The dacoits were bands of armed pirates who preyed on boats going up and down the river. One band of dacoits tried to swoop in and raid the boat Adoniram and James Colman were traveling on, but the crew fended them off by firing a volley of gunshots over their heads. Since no one knew whether they or other bands of dacoits would try to attack again, the month-long trip to Ava was tense.

lived & dacoits in abandoned city

Finally, though, on January 25, 1820, as Adoniram looked out over the elaborate dragon-head shaped bow of the boat, he saw the golden steeple of the royal palace come into view. Soon the boat was safely tied up at the river's edge in Ava.

Adoniram and James Colman spent the next day trying to obtain permission for an audience with the king. This would have turned out to be an impossible task, except for one thing: Mya-day-men, the old viceroy of Rangoon. The viceroy was now the highest-ranking official in King Bagyidaw's court, and although he had never been great friends with Adoniram, Mya-day-men's wife, the vice-reine, had been a particularly good friend of Ann's. As a result, the viceroy agreed to help Adoniram get an audience with the king. Later that night, a messenger arrived at the boat with a letter telling Adoniram that he and James Colman could have an audience with the king the following day.

There was no sleep for the two missionaries that night. They both lay on their straw mats on the deck of the boat praying and talking. The future direction of Christianity in Burma hung in the balance. The following day they would know which way the balance would tip.

Both men were up at sunrise. They each had special clothes made for the occasion of entering the Golden Presence, as having an audience with the king was called. It had been difficult to know what to wear, but in the end they had decided on long robes like those the Buddhist monks wore, only theirs were white, not the distinctive saffron color of the monks' robes. Adoniram hoped the robes would remind the king that they were "priests," just not Buddhist ones.

settling

! ! Gold Leaf Bibles For the king

Dust from the unpaved streets swirled around Adoniram and James Colman as they made their way to the Golden Palace. Each of them carried three volumes of the Bible. Adoniram had paid a lot of money to have the cover of each Bible overlaid in gold leaf as a suitable gift for the king. When they reached the guardhouse set into the outer wall of the palace, a guard ordered them to remove their shoes. He then ushered them into the outer corridor.

Once the men were in the outer corridor, one of the many officials milling around beckoned them into a large hall. Adoniram gasped as he entered. Every inch of the room, and everything in it—the chair, the pillars, the fans—was made of gold. There were twelve Burmese men standing in the room. Adoniram supposed some were servants and others important dignitaries who had come for an audience with the king as well.

setting

Suddenly there was a commotion at the far end of the room, and a servant ran in. "The golden feet are proceeding this way!" he yelled as he dove onto the carpeted floor. Every Burmese man in the room followed his example, each lying face down, his face flat against the floor.

Bow to king

Adoniram looked at James Colman. "I suppose it would be proper to kneel before a monarch," he said, sinking to his knees. James Colman followed his example.

! ! viceroy

A minute later a short, bandy-legged man wearing a white muslin tunic with a scarlet waistband and a turban wound around his head entered the room.

dignitaries

Complete silence followed. Not one of the men prostrate on the floor moved a muscle.

The short man, whom Adoniram knew without a doubt was King Bagyidaw, glared at the two white men kneeling in front of him.

"Who are these men?" he demanded.

Adoniram decided it would be best to answer for himself. He bowed his head slightly and replied, "We are the religious teachers you have heard about, O great king."

King Bagyidaw looked shocked. "You speak like a Burmese man. How can this be? What have you come for?"

The official who had the petition for the king lifted his head off the carpet and spoke quietly. "If it please you, your majesty, the men have a petition they would like to bring before you."

"Then read it," commanded the king, settling himself onto his golden throne.

The official slid the petition in front of his eyes and, still lying flat on the floor, began to read. "The American teachers present themselves to receive the favor of the excellent king, the sovereign of land and sea. Hearing that on account of the greatness of the royal power, the royal country was in a quiet and prosperous state...."

As the official read on, Adoniram watched the king's face for any sign of what he might be thinking. At least the king seemed to be paying attention.

The official read on about how the missionaries had come from Rangoon to Ava to ask for royal permission to tell the Burmese people about their religion free from government harassment. When the official was finished, the king beckoned for the paper. Adoniram watched in amazement as the official crawled on his belly up to the throne and handed the petition to the king.

The king carefully reread the petition. "Do you have any examples of this religion?" he asked Adoniram.

Adoniram rummaged around in the pocket of his robe and pulled out one of his tracts, which he handed to the king. King Bagyidaw read the first line and dropped the leaflet. It fluttered slowly to the floor. A chill went through Adoniram; this was not a good sign.

The king glared at the two missionaries, and Adoniram did not know what to say next. Thankfully, the courtier who had been holding the six Bibles rose to a crawling position, and shuffling the books in front of him, he presented them to the king. "Take them away," said King Bagyidaw. "I have no use for foreign religious books in my realm." With that he stood and walked out of the room.

Once the king was gone, everyone scrambled to his feet and hurried out. No one looked at Adoniram or James Colman, except the official with the petition. "You must leave now, quickly!" the official said, pushing the men through the golden door. "The king is not pleased with your petition. You must go."

Determined

Chapter 14

A Growing Band of Believers

B y the time Adoniram and James Colman returned to Rangoon on February 18, 1820, Adoniram was convinced of what he should do. He and Ann would leave Burma as soon as possible and set up a mission station somewhere else. He thought Chittagong might be a suitable location, especially since the lone missionary to the Burmese people living there had been murdered. The fledgling church the missionary had started there was now without a leader. Of course, Adoniram would be sad to leave Rangoon, but he knew it was the best thing to do for the sake of the three Burmese converts. Now that King Bagyidaw had turned his back on Christianity, anyone who had contact with the missionaries would be putting his life in jeopardy.

February 18, 1820

!!
idea to mov to Chitt with Ann TQ

159

Several days after returning from Ava, Adoniram laid out his plan to the tiny group of Burmese Christians. He expected them to be relieved that they would no longer have to associate with foreigners during this period of the king's displeasure, but the opposite was the case.

"Don't leave us yet," begged Maung Byaay.

"But it's useless for me to stay," Adoniram replied sadly, thinking about how he had taught Maung Byaay to read and write, and about how much Maung Byaay loved to study the Bible with Adoniram. "We cannot open the zayat. No Burmese person will want to inquire about Christianity now that people know that the king is displeased with us. It's better for Ann and me to go and come back when circumstances change and you are no longer in danger because of your association with us."

"No, no," insisted Maung Byaay. "Stay with us until there are eight or ten Christians here. Then you can train one of us to be the leader and you can leave. We will not be worried then, because even if you left the country, the religion you preach would spread itself. Why, even the king could not stop it. But if you go now, what would happen if someone wants to join our religion? I could not baptize him. What would we do?"

Although Adoniram was very moved by the argument, he was not persuaded. After all, he had just been to Ava and had seen firsthand the king and the power he exerted over people. But he could not dismiss what Maung Byaay had said without promising to give the matter some consideration.

TQ

While Adoniram was considering what to do, the three Burmese Christians were acting. They talked to everyone they could think of about their faith, and on the following Sunday, each of them brought to church one man who was "willing to consider" the religion of the foreigners.

!!

More believers

Risky

Although none of the men became converts, Adoniram was greatly encouraged by their presence. The men had dared to enter the mission house for a church service, and they had asked some searching questions during the service. Their presence had the desired effect. Adoniram and Ann decided it would be wrong of them to leave the struggling little church in Rangoon, even if their going meant that the local Christians would be safer from reprisals by government officials.

TQ

Yet the small group of Burmese Christians in Chittagong needed a leader, and so it was decided that James Colman and his wife should move there. In Chittagong they could help the struggling church and maintain a safe haven for the Judsons and the Burmese Christians to flee to if things turned really ugly in Rangoon.

Plan = James moves to Chittag.

Backup Plan

By the end of March, Adoniram and Ann were once again the only missionaries in Rangoon. This time, though, they had three local converts for company. And these new Christians kept active. Soon two wealthy Burmese men had also become Christians and asked to be baptized. A third

March only mission. + 3 Christians + 2

reprisals — James & wife should move to Chittagong

Maung Shway-gnong

man, Maung Shway-gnong, was also very close to accepting the gospel. However, he hung back, afraid. Maung Shway-gnong was a well-respected Buddhist scholar, and his conversion would stun the religious leaders in Rangoon. There was little doubt in Adoniram's mind that if Maung Shway-gnong were to become a Christian he would be put to death immediately.

The growing group of converts and interested people was all a surprise to Adoniram. Although Adoniram had arrived back from Ava convinced that his missionary work in Burma was over, now it was thriving. He couldn't have been more pleased, except for one thing. Ann's health was getting worse by the day. Adoniram knew that Ann needed to see a doctor, but there wasn't one in Rangoon. The closest place with a good doctor was Calcutta, India. So Adoniram booked passage for himself and Ann on the first ship leaving Rangoon for Calcutta. He was reluctant to leave his missionary work, especially now that things were going so well, but Ann was too ill to travel alone.

Before he and Ann left, Adoniram baptized the two newest converts, Maung Shway-gnong, the Buddhist scholar, and Mah Men-lay, the first woman convert. The baptisms were held at dusk in a quiet pool just outside the mission house gates. As he baptized Maung Shway-gnong, Adoniram wondered whether he would see him alive again. He supposed the religious and government leaders

Mah Men-lay

would conspire to have Maung Shway-gnong killed *setting* lest other Burmese people follow his example.

On July 19, 1820, Adoniram and Ann Judson set *July 19, 1820* sail from Rangoon. It was the first time Ann had been outside of Burma since arriving there seven years before. In that time, both she and Adoniram had worked hard, and now as they left, ten Burmese *10 christian converts* Christian converts lined the dock to bid them farewell. Adoniram did not know what lay ahead for these Christians, but he prayed that Maung Byaay *TQ prayed 4 them* had been right and that a church with ten members could not be destroyed by the most determined of kings.

In the Bay of Bengal, the winds were favorable, allowing the captain to shave several days off the normal one-month sailing time from Rangoon to Calcutta. Once in Calcutta, Adoniram wasted no time finding the best doctor in the city for Ann. Dr. Chalmers diagnosed Ann's illness as liver disease *Ann = liver disease* and blamed the condition on the heat and poor diet they endured in Rangoon. He recommended Ann return to the United States for a rest, but she would not hear of it. She insisted her place was with her *Ann = determind* husband in Burma.

After three months in Calcutta, Ann had recovered enough to return to Rangoon. Regrettably, the *Full recovery ship back* voyage back was not nearly as pleasant as the trip to Calcutta had been. The ship was infested with scorpions, and it ran into the worst lightning storms *scorpion infested* Adoniram had ever experienced. It was six grueling weeks before the ship was piloted up the Rangoon

River. Adoniram and Ann stood on deck and held hands as the golden spires of the Shwe Dagon pagoda once again loomed above them. For better or worse, they were home.

Home

All of the Judson's Burmese converts were there to meet them, including Maung Shway-gnong. After the couple had cleared customs, everyone went back to the mission house, where Adoniram and Ann caught up on all the news. The most import- ant piece was that Mya-day-men, the old viceroy of Rangoon, was back, and holding the same position. It was wonderful news, especially for Ann, who had been a good friend of the vicereine. Adoniram and Ann thanked God that once again they had a sympathetic ear in government circles. Indeed, this favor had already proved helpful. News of Maung Shway-gnong's conversion had been brought to the viceroy's attention by informants who had hoped the traitor would be put to death as a warning to others who might want to convert to Christianity. Instead of reacting, the viceroy had just shrugged and told the informants he was not interested in hearing any more about the matter. As a result, Maung Shway-gnong was alive and well and more enthusiastic than ever about the new faith he had embraced.

Some news, though, was not so good. King Bagyidaw had decided to declare war on neighbor- ing Siam. Over thirty thousand troops had marched through Rangoon on their way to the border. No one could predict when or how the war would end.

!! / Christians / are alive

Mya-day-men / (viceroy) / (vicereine's / husband)

!!

viceroy / = saved / Shway

setting / war w / neighbors

Everyone would just have to wait patiently to see what the final outcome would be.

Despite a border war, there was more to do than ever for Adoniram and Ann. With ten church members, there were Bible studies to hold, reading and writing classes to conduct for women and girls, and the ongoing task of translating the Bible into the Burmese language.

— Busy A3A

Not long after his return from Calcutta, Adoniram received more encouragement. It came in the form of Maung Yah, the first Burmese man he had ever heard speak about the existence of an eternal God. Soon after Maung Yah had visited the mission house, he had been transferred to a government post hundreds of miles away. Now he was back in Rangoon, and he wasted no time in visiting Adoniram. He explained that he had read all the printed material Adoniram had given him until he knew it by heart—and believed it. Now he too wanted to become a part of the church.

— Yah wants to convert

Adoniram was overjoyed. The seeds of the gospel he had planted in the hearts of Burmese people were beginning to sprout. It was more important than ever that he carry on with the Bible translation work. In July 1821, he completed translating the four Gospels and the letters from John. He moved on to the Book of Acts, but sickness held him up time after time. First it was a bout of cholera, then a series of other tropical diseases. And Ann, too, was very sick again. So sick, in fact, that Adoniram feared for her life. It was clear she needed to get back to the United

!! ^ 1821 translated 4 gospels 3 letters A&A sickness = setback

States for proper medical help. Adoniram's younger brother <u>Elnathan was now a surgeon</u> in Boston, and Adoniram wanted Ann to go there so that he could treat her.

Ann agreed this time, and arrangements were made. She caught the first ship out of Rangoon bound for Calcutta, where she transferred to another ship for the voyage to Boston. It broke Adoniram's heart to see his wife leave. In a letter he described the feeling as being as painful and crippling as having his right arm amputated. He would not see Ann for at least two years, if she was well enough to come back at all.

Adoniram toiled on alone until <u>December 1821,</u> when another missionary family—<u>Jonathan and Hope Price</u>—sent out by the <u>American Baptist mission</u> joined him in Rangoon. <u>Jonathan Price</u> was a doctor, and Adoniram welcomed him with open arms. Dr. Price was a tall, skinny man with a shock of white-blond hair. The Burmese flocked around the mission house for a glimpse of him. Dr. Price was not one bit shy, and he laughed as the local people poked him and tugged at his hair to see whether it was a wig. Within weeks, he was a popular figure in Rangoon, trying to talk Burmese as he tended to the medical needs of people. He was especially fond of cutting out cataracts, the milky white growth that sometimes covers the eyes of older people. No one else in all Burma knew how to remove cataracts, and soon people were coming hundreds of miles to have their eyes operated on by Dr. Price.

Although Jonathan Price flourished in Rangoon, his wife did not. Despite all her husband's best medical treatment, Hope Price died of dysentery six weeks after arriving in Burma. A second grave was dug under the mango tree in the mission house yard beside the grave of little Roger Judson.

Hope = dead

About the same time, the Houghs returned to Rangoon with the printing press. They had met Ann in Calcutta on her way to the United States and as a result had decided to move back to Rangoon to support Adoniram, who was delighted to see them.

Hough return w/ press
Ann in Calcutta persuaded Houghs to come back

Six months later, Dr. Price received a summons to appear before King Bagyidaw in Ava. Adoniram hated to leave Rangoon, but he could see no other option but to go along with him. Jonathan Price did not know enough Burmese to appear alone before the king. One slip of his tongue and his head could be ordered cut off.

Ad. has to go

In early October the two missionaries finally made it to Ava and found themselves bowing before King Bagyidaw. All went well. The king wanted to know all about Jonathan Price's cataract operations. Adoniram served as interpreter. When the king had finally exhausted all his questions, he ordered, "Stay in Ava. I might require your services."

2 Oct. Have to stay in Ava

Adoniram's heart sank. There was no way they could return to Rangoon against a direct order from the king. Who knew how long they might be in Ava? The only thing Adoniram could be thankful for was that the Houghs were in Rangoon looking after the band of new Christians.

can't return to Rangoon

Adoniram tried to make the most of his extended visit to Ava. He found it a little unnerving being right under King Bagyidaw's nose, but he spoke privately with many Burmese people, including the king's brother, Prince Mong, about Christianity. The prince had somehow survived the slaughter that occurred when his brother ascended to the throne. To Adoniram's surprise, some members of the royal family encouraged him in his missionary work. Princess Sarawady, the king's youngest sister, even hinted that King Bagyidaw was considering giving him land on which to build a *kyoung*, the Burmese word for a holy house.

All of this was cause for excitement. Ava was an important city with 700,000 people living in and around it. If the king finally recognized him as a holy man, Adoniram would have free access to preach and teach in Ava and anywhere else in the country.

In the meantime, Dr. Price was furthering his reputation as an excellent surgeon. Cataract surgery could be risky, however, and on one particular occasion, his knife slipped during an operation, causing his female patient to become blind. Dr. Price felt so sorry for her that he married her on the spot so that he could take care of her.

Adoniram was horrified. His missionary partner had just married a Buddhist woman without so much as discussing the matter with him. To make things worse, Adoniram had just learned that James Colman, who had left Rangoon to work among the Burmese living in Chittagong, had died of disease.

And if that weren't enough, he hadn't heard anything from Ann in over eight months.

Adoniram longed to get back to the little church in Rangoon, but he could not leave Ava without royal permission. He just hoped that permission wasn't too long in coming.

Ann = no response in 8mo

Chapter 15

Called by the King

It was January 25, 1823, before Adoniram was issued a permit to return to Rangoon, where he had also been given permission to build a kyo-ung. He started making plans. He would return to Rangoon and check up on the state of the new church and build the kyoung while he waited for Ann to return from the United States. The two of them would then move to Ava. By now, Adoniram had made many friends in Ava and had a good grasp on the inner workings of the government. Both of these things convinced him that one day he would have the opportunity to openly preach the gospel in the royal city. Jonathan Price would stay on in Ava while Adoniram was away.

[handwritten margin notes: "!! can go back to Rangoon", "Ad. knows Ava & ppl well", "John is still in Ava"]

Kyoung

When he finally got back to Rangoon, Adoniram found some things to be encouraged about and other things that were disheartening. Mah Menlay, the first woman convert, had died. Many of the homes of other converts had been burned down, or the people had been driven out of their neighborhoods in retaliation for becoming Christians. Adoniram did what he could to help these new believers. He also continued his translation work and made plans to build the kyoung. All the while he waited for news of Ann.

Finally, much to his relief, Adoniram received word that Ann was sailing back to Rangoon and he could expect her to arrive sometime in December. Accompanying her on the voyage were two new missionaries, Jonathan and Deborah Wade. Adoniram could hardly wait. He had missed his wife so much, and he looked forward to having her at his side again. He was also delighted that the Wades were coming. The timing was perfect. Since he had decided to move to Ava with Ann, the Wades would be able to work alongside the Houghs in Rangoon.

Sure enough, right on schedule, Ann and the Wades arrived safely in Rangoon. After giving Jonathan and Deborah Wade several days of orientation to the work of the mission and life in Burma, Adoniram and Ann set out for Ava.

The trip upriver against the current was particularly slow, but that did not matter to Adoniram and Ann. They had so much to catch up on. Ann had news from his family. Adoniram's father had resigned his position as a Congregational Church pastor and had become a Baptist. His younger brother Elnathan was a prominent government surgeon and he had insisted that Ann return to Burma with the small table and rocking chair he had bought for her.

Ann also showed her husband a copy of a book called *An Account of the American Baptist Mission to the Burman Empire.* Ann had written it herself, and the book had been published in the United States. Adoniram was greatly impressed; his wife had done a masterful job with the writing. Ann also had a letter for Adoniram from Brown University, where he had gone to college. The letter stated that Adoniram had been given an honorary Doctorate of Divinity, which meant that he could use the title of doctor and call himself Doctor Judson.

Six weeks after setting out, their boat finally arrived on the outskirts of Ava. Adoniram spotted Jonathan Price paddling a small boat towards them. When he got nearer, Jonathan explained that the conflict between the Burmese and the British was getting worse every day. Things had reached the point where any foreigner in Ava, whether British or American, was looked on with suspicion. Undeterred, Adoniram decided to stay. As far as he was concerned, it was too late to turn back now. Besides, what happened in Ava would most likely happen in other places in the kingdom, including Rangoon.

The Judsons moved into a small hut while Adoniram set about building a more permanent mission house next door. The house was made of brick to try to keep out some of the stifling heat of Ava. It had three rooms and a large veranda that ran the length of the house.

Adoniram went to visit his old friends at the royal court, but he soon found out that many of them had left and those who were still there did not want to see him. It would have been a very lonely time for him if Ann had not been with him. Ann kept herself busy taking care of three small girls whose mother had gone insane and abandoned them.

Ann = sweet

Several European visitors living in Ava kept Adoniram informed on what was happening in the city. One of these visitors was Henry Gouger, whose company Adoniram enjoyed very much. Although Henry Gouger was only in his mid-twenties, he had a knack for making money. He had brought a shipload of goods from Europe and sold them at a huge profit in Burma. This had made him a very rich man. He soon found out, however, that Burmese law forbade any gold or jewels from leaving the country, and since they were the currency used to pay for things in Burma, Henry had no way of getting his new fortune home. Still, Henry Gouger was an optimistic man who believed that sooner or later he would find a way to get his money out of the country.

Throughout the next year, rumors continued to spread about what the British were up to on Burma's

veranda   Henry Gouger — trader rich

border with India. On Sunday evening, <u>May 23,</u> <u>1824,</u> the rumors turned to fact. A fleet of British warships sailed upriver to Rangoon and bombarded the city. After a brave fight, the locals abandoned the city, and a British captain raised the Union Jack over the docks. Great Britain and Burma were at war!

At first the Burmese people in Ava didn't believe that foreigners had entered their country. Then they decided they had but it was all part of a clever trap. The great Burmese army could not be defeated! What must have happened, they told one another, was that the army had lured the British far upriver so that they could be captured and used as slaves. Indeed, many officials in Ava began putting in "orders" for slaves. One man requested "six white strangers to row my boat." Another woman commented that she would like two or three white men because she had heard they made intelligent servants. The Burmese were unable to grasp the truth of the situation: A power existed in the world that was greater than the king, their Golden Ruler. As the days passed, however, the Burmese came to understand that the British were powerful and meant business. A gloom settled over the kingdom.

About this time, Adoniram heard some disturbing news: Henry Gouger had been arrested and interrogated. The Burmese had found some maps among his belongings, simple sketches he had drawn to help him find his way around Ava. To the Burmese officials interrogating him the maps were evidence that Henry Gouger was a spy. Worse, the officials also found receipts showing that Henry Gouger had paid Adoniram several large sums of money, implicating Adoniram as a co-conspirator.

Of course, Adoniram was no spy, and neither was Henry Gouger. What had really happened was that Henry Gouger had helped Adoniram get money from the Baptist mission fund in the United States through the bank that Henry dealt with in Calcutta. Adoniram knew that the Burmese officials would not believe this. As far as they were concerned, he was a spy. He waited to see what would happen next.

On Tuesday, June 8, 1824, Adoniram and Ann were just about to sit down to dinner together when the door to their house burst open and twelve Burmese men surged inside. Adoniram put down the bowl of curry he was carrying to the table and stepped forward. "What is it you want?" he asked, glancing around quickly to make sure Ann stayed behind him.

A man carrying a large black book glared at him. Like the eleven other men, he had a spot the size of a silver dollar tattooed on each cheek. Adoniram realized grimly that the distinctive mark on the faces of these men meant only one thing: The men were the dreaded Spotted Faces, criminals who should have died for their crimes but who were spared to become the executioners and thugs who ran Burma's prisons. Many of the Spotted Faces also had their crimes tattooed on their foreheads or chests. The spots on their cheeks made it

BRAVE

impossible for them to escape from the hell they created for themselves and their prisoners.

"We have come for the teacher," snarled the man with the book.

"That's me," replied Adoniram, marveling at how calm he managed to sound.

"You are called by the king," said the man.

Fear gripped Adoniram. Being called by the king was the Burmese way of placing a person under arrest. Immediately the group of Spotted Faces pounced on Adoniram and punched him to the ground. Adoniram felt a thin cord being wrapped around his arms above his elbows and then yanked tight. He let out a gasp of pain as the cord ripped through his skin. He felt blood seep through his shirtsleeve.

[margin note: Ad. was beaten & bound by the Spotted Faces = going to Burmese prison]

Ann sprang forward. "Stop," she begged. "Don't hurt him. I will give you money."

Adoniram groaned at what he heard next.

"Take her too," barked the chief Spotted Face. "She is foreign also."

[margin note: CC they took Ann]

Adoniram struggled to his knees. "Don't take her unless her name is written in the book," he pleaded, fearing Ann would not survive more than a few nights in a Burmese prison, especially since she had just found out she was pregnant again. *[margin note: A♀A]*

The Spotted Face grunted and turned his attention back to Adoniram. With a final twist of the cord, he ordered him dragged outside and off to the courthouse. As Adoniram stumbled out the door he could hear Ann crying behind him. The pain of the cords biting into his skin was excruciating for Adoniram, but nothing like the pain he felt inside at having to leave Ann alone without protection.

Half walking, half dragged, Adoniram arrived at the courthouse, where the governor of Ava stood waiting for him. He had no trial, no opportunity to ask why he was there, only a verdict. "Guilty," declared the governor. "Send him to Let-may-yoon."

Let-may-yoon meant the Death Prison. It had the reputation of being the most vicious prison in Burma, and as he rumbled along in a cart toward the prison, Adoniram wondered how he would survive there.

The head Spotted Face of the prison stood waiting for Adoniram at the gate. "Welcome, my son," he said, his malicious smile revealing a row of broken yellow teeth. Adoniram cringed as he noticed the words tattooed on the man's bare chest: Loo-that, murderer. "We are one big happy family in here," he continued. "Everyone calls me 'Aphe.'"

Adoniram tried to nod, but Aphe meant father, and he could think of no one on earth less like a father than this man.

"Come with me. I have a surprise for you," said Aphe, pulling Adoniram out of the wagon. He then commanded a Spotted Face with his ears cut off to take him to a huge block of granite in the center of the prison yard. There Adoniram had three pairs of fetters riveted closed around his ankles.

"Try to walk now," laughed Aphe, "and see how far you get."

setting

Adoniram obediently stood and took a step. The fetters pulled at his ankles, causing him to fall flat on his face in the dust.

The courtyard erupted into laughter. "Take him to his cell," ordered Aphe when he finally stopped laughing.

Adoniram found himself being dragged again, this time down a ~~musty~~ corridor until he was finally dumped in a windowless cell.

put in a crowded cell

After the door closed behind him, Adoniram twisted the fetters so that they did not cut into his skin. He then looked around the cell. His eyes had not yet adjusted to the darkness, but he could sense other prisoners in the room. He could smell them, too. The stench of human waste and rotting flesh was overpowering. Finally he began to make out some shapes in the darkness, and then the shapes slowly became the outlines of people he knew. Henry Gouger was lying against the far wall, and the Scottish sea captain he had once met, Captain Laird, was slumped over in the corner. Neither man spoke.

Henry Gouger & Capt. Laird

Others were in the room too, about fifty people in all, mainly men, but a few women. They were all spread around on the teakwood floor of the cell. Some of the other prisoners groaned softly, and one or two mumbled Buddhist prayers.

As the tiny amount of light that filtered into the cell from the outside gave way to darkness, Adoniram wondered what night would be like in the cell. It turned out to be worse than anything he could have imagined. About an hour after Adoniram

TQ

musty

was dumped in the cell, the door creaked open again, and Dr. Price was thrown inside. Aphe and two other Spotted Faces followed him in. Adoniram watched in horror as they lowered a bamboo pole from the ceiling and hooked each prisoner's fetters to it. Then they hoisted the pole into the air until it was four feet off the ground. Adoniram lay with the others, half hanging from the pole. His feet were four feet in the air, with only his shoulders and head touching the floor.

Aphe chuckled to himself. "That will keep you all safe for the night," he said as he lit the oil lamp in the middle of the room. "Sleep well, my children." With that he turned and marched out of the cell. One of the other Spotted Faces slammed the door shut behind him and locked it.

Now that the prisoners were sure they were alone, they whispered to each other long into the night. The Burmese man to the right of Henry Gouger told them how he had seen foreigners being tortured and beaten to death. Adoniram learned from Henry Gouger that he had spent two weeks in stocks before being thrown into the cell and that King Bagyidaw had declared all foreigners to be spies. It seemed only a matter of time before they would all be dead. After a few hours in the wretched cell, Adoniram began to hope that death would come quickly.

Finally the cell fell silent except for an occasional groan and the rustling of rats as they scurried between the rows of dangling prisoners.

Adoniram tried not to think about what might be happening at home. Had Ann been arrested? Was she strung up in some other cell right now? And what about the New Testament he had just finished translating? It was in a drawer of his desk. It would surely be burned, probably along with the whole house. Slowly Adoniram's thoughts became as hopeless as the human misery around him. He wondered whether all his efforts in Burma had been for nothing.

The following day went much as Adoniram had expected it would. Aphe came in early in the morning and lowered the bamboo pole. The prisoners were all unhitched from it and taken out in small groups for a ten-minute walk around the courtyard. It was the only time Adoniram saw daylight that day. The stench of human waste, along with that of decaying flesh, made going back into the cell almost unbearable.

The cell had another smell, that of of rotting food. The Spotted Faces did not provide any food for the inmates of the jail. Those without family or friends on the outside to deliver food to them were doomed to die of starvation. On certain religious days, though, Buddhist women would bring ngapi and rice to the prison to give to the prisoners. Ngapi, a fish paste, smelled bad enough when it was fresh, but after it had been wrapped in banana leaves and "saved" for a week or two, it stank beyond description. Many prisoners kept a stack of leaves smeared with ngapi stacked against the cell wall, though Adoniram could not believe they ate it without gagging.

It was two days before Ann came to visit him. She arrived with food and an order from the city governor written on a palm leaf that allowed her to enter the prison. Adoniram had lost much of his strength, and he half walked, half crawled to the doorway. He wondered what Ann would say when she saw him. In all their eleven years of marriage, Ann had never seen him look or smell so foul.

Through the bars in the door, Adoniram could see Ann silhouetted against the wall. When she saw him, she buried her head in her hands and sobbed.

"Ann," he said weakly, "thank God you are all right."

Ann looked at her husband and forced a smile. "I'll find a way to get you out of here," she said. "I already have the city governor working on your behalf. And I brought you some food."

They talked quietly for a few minutes until a Spotted Face ordered Ann to leave immediately. Ann's pleas made no difference, nor did the order from the governor permitting her to be in the prison.

Adoniram watched hopelessly as Ann was roughly escorted to the gate. He wondered whether he would ever see her again.

Chapter 16

Oung-pen-la

A nn visited Adoniram whenever she could persuade the Spotted Faces to let her into the prison. Each visit made Adoniram more concerned for her safety. Burmese officials had ransacked the house, removing anything of value. Ann had anticipated they might do this, and so she had buried some gold and Adoniram's complete translation of the New Testament in the garden. The gold could stay there forever, but the paper on which the translation was written would soon rot. The translation had taken years to painstaking work to complete, and Ann asked Adoniram what she should do to keep it safe.

Adoniram thought for several days about what to do with the translation. He had no friends on

183

the outside he could trust. They were all in prison with him. Even if he did have friends he could trust, he would not put them in such danger. To be found with foreign documents would mean certain death for a Burmese person. In the end, Adoniram asked Ann to sew the pages of the translation into a pillow—not just any pillow, but the lumpiest, dirtiest pillow she could find—and bring it to him. That way he could have the translation under his nose at all times, and with any luck the pillow would be too repulsive for even the greediest Spotted Face to want.

The days dragged into weeks, and the prisoners waited for something, anything, to happen. Occasionally, they would hear a single shot fired from a Burmese gunboat on the nearby river. This was a signal for the city that the Burmese army had lost another round of fighting to the British. It was also a warning to the foreign prisoners that there would be no visitors, no talking, and no walks in the sunlight for the next few days.

Eventually Ann's persistence at trying to get someone in an official position to help Adoniram and the other foreign prisoners paid off. The prisoners were all moved to tiny day sheds, small bamboo huts in the prison courtyard where they could sit during daylight hours. It was an enormous relief to Adoniram to be out of the cell and in the fresh air. Regrettably, it also brought him closer to the screams of prisoners being tortured throughout the day. He hated to hear the screaming, but he learned to put up with it because being outside was much better than being locked up twenty-four hours a day in a stinking, rat-infested, overcrowded cell. At night, the prisoners were returned to the cell to be hoisted up by their feet on the bamboo shaft.

The hours when Ann was not visiting dragged for Adoniram, who passed the time playing chess. He had always loved the game but had seldom had the time to play it since arriving in Burma. Now he had all the time in the world. He and Henry Gouger made a set of chess pieces from slivers of bamboo. They used soot from the oil lamp in their cell to draw a chessboard on an old piece of cowhide a dead Burmese prisoner had left behind. Adoniram and Henry played chess for hours each day.

When Ann had to stop visiting him, Adoniram was particularly glad of the distraction of chess. Ann was due to have the baby any day, and Adoniram worried constantly about the birth. Ann had already lost two children, and it was more than he could bear to think of her losing a third.

On January 26, 1825, a messenger slipped a note through the cell door to Adoniram. "Maria Elizabeth Butterworth Judson born today. Thank God we are both alive. Love Ann," it read.

Relief washed over Adoniram, but the feeling was soon replaced with waves of sadness. What lay ahead for little Maria? Would she ever see her father? Would she and her mother be killed if the British army came any closer to Ava? As Adoniram sat fettered in his day shed in the prison courtyard, he could not predict what lay ahead for his little family. He could only pray that the future would be less bleak than the present.

It was March first when things changed dramatically in the prison. In the late afternoon, a group of Spotted Faces surrounded the day shed that Adoniram was lying in. "Get up now and go inside," growled the largest Spotted Face.

Adoniram's chains jangled as he crawled from the shed, clutching his pillow with the Burmese translation of the New Testament inside.

"Leave that there," the Spotted Face commanded, poking at the filthy pillow with a stick.

Adoniram left the pillow and began walking. He was nearly across the courtyard before he turned around. What he saw sent terror through him. The Spotted Faces were whacking at the hut with long sticks. Before he ducked his head to go into the inner prison, Adoniram took one last look. The shed was now a pile of broken pieces of bamboo lying on the ground, and in the middle of the pile was the pillow that held the precious translation. Dejected, Adoniram walked back into the cell.

Once inside, Adoniram wondered what was happening. Had the British arrived in Ava? Once he was seated in his usual spot on the teakwood floor with his back resting against the cracked wall, Adoniram soon heard the rumors that were being whispered around. The most persistent one was that they were all to be executed at three in the morning. As if to confirm this, the sound of knives being sharpened started up outside their cell.

(handwritten margin notes: pray; March 1st; L! Has to leave pillow; CC why did they tear down the hut?; pillow is in the rubble; TQ L! All might be executed)

(handwritten note at bottom: Word got out that they're all to be executed at 3am)

"Thank goodness," muttered Henry Gouger. "I was worried we might be strangled. A slit throat isn't such a bad end compared to some of the ways I've seen people die in here."

Adoniram nodded in agreement. They would all be thankful if they died quickly without being tortured first.

At 3 A.M. the door to the cell clanked open, and a group of toothless Spotted Faces appeared. Some of the prisoners began to yell and scream. Others sobbed quietly. Adoniram and Henry looked knowingly at each other and waited for the inevitable. The bamboo pole was lowered, and only the foreign men were unchained from it and ordered to form a line and march outside.

It had been many months since Adoniram had been outside at night. The cooler evening air seemed to embrace him. At least if he was going to die, it would be with fresh air filling his lungs.

The prisoners were led to the slab of granite in the center of the courtyard. This was where Adoniram's fetters had been riveted together around his ankles when he had arrived at the prison. Adoniram thought it would make a good chopping block as he waited for the final order to be given to execute the prisoners. It never came. Instead, Aphe himself barked an order from behind them. "Put two more sets of fetters on each prisoner."

Adoniram looked around, puzzled. Why would they be having two extra sets of leg irons put on them if they were going to die?

The hammering of rivets continued until day-break. The prisoners were then returned to their cell, where they tried to work out what the last twenty-four hours might mean for them.

Things never returned to "normal" after that. The eight foreign prisoners were kept in the inner cell and were not allowed to go outside except for a few brief minutes in the middle of the night. Since they had not been killed, Adoniram began to fret about the fate of the pillow containing the translation of the New Testament. Would he ever see it again? If he survived this wretched ordeal, would there be a manuscript to publish, or would he have to start all over again with his translation work? He wished he knew what had happened to the pillow.

The way the foreign prisoners were being treated made no sense to Adoniram, at least not until Ann, who was still able to visit, told him what was happening outside the prison.

The war was going badly for the Burmese, who were no match for the disciplined ranks of British soldiers with their superior weapons. Ann had visited the governor of the city so many times to plead for Adoniram's life that the two of them had become good friends. The governor was fascinated with America and American ways, and he spent hours plying Ann with questions and listening to stories of her childhood. In return, he agreed to do whatever he could for the foreign prisoners, though since they had been jailed under direct order of the king, he could not secure their release.

[Handwritten margin notes: "TQ — prisoners are confused", ""normal"", "LI", "Ad. worried about the pillow", "TQ", "Reports to Ann", "setting", "!!", "Ann pleads to gov. to release", "foreigners = worried", "Got governor to agree, but not king"]

The queen's brother, Prince Menthagee, had a particular hatred for foreigners, and he had hinted three times that the foreign prisoners should all be killed. The governor had ignored his suggestions, but he knew that if an order came in writing he would have no choice but to obey it. In an attempt to keep the foreigner prisoners alive, he had banished them all back to their inner cell, where few people would see them. He told Ann he hoped that once they were out of sight the prince would forget about them.

Things stayed this way until May 2, 1825, when the doors to the cell were flung open again.

"Get up. We are moving you," yelled Aphe, the head Spotted Face.

By now Adoniram had been in prison for eleven months, and even if he had not been suffering from fever, he would hardly have had the strength to pull himself up from the wooden floor. Henry Gouger helped him.

"I wonder where we're…" began Henry.

"Silence," yelled Aphe, reinforcing his command by cracking his whip across Henry's back.

The prisoners stood in line and shuffled silently out the door. Outside, each man waited as his fetters were chiseled off. Then all eight of the prisoners were roped together in pairs and prodded with spears as they were herded through the prison gate.

Adoniram was roped to Captain Laird, the Scottish sea captain who had been a stocky, strong man before being thrown in jail. Now the captain was bent over, weak, and haggard from his months of mistreatment in prison.

The road the men were marched down led to the courthouse. As the prisoners stumbled along, men and women on the side of the road turned their heads away. Only the children stopped to stare at the four pairs of walking dead.

At the courthouse, the prisoners stood in one-hundred-degree heat as official custody of them was handed over to the commander of Lamaing province, which led Adoniram to believe they were about to take a journey. He was right. They were to travel eight miles on foot, wearing no shoes, and with feet tender from eleven months of sitting in a darkened cell.

The commander rode on in front of the prisoners. The Spotted Faces, their long spears ready to prod anyone who fell, walked beside the men. They had scarcely gone a hundred yards when Adoniram's feet began to blister from the hot bricks that paved the street around the courthouse. Half a mile later, the procession of filthy, emaciated prisoners shuffled across the Mootangai Bridge. For a fleeting moment, Adoniram thought about throwing himself off the bridge and onto the rocks below. His death would be quick and sure, unlike the endless nightmare he was now living. But he was roped to Captain Laird, so even escape through death was not an option for Adoniram.

Another half mile farther on, one of the prisoners, a Greek man, collapsed. The Spotted Faces beat him mercilessly, but not surprising, this did not help him to get up and walk any farther. Finally, the commander ordered a cart to be sent for him, and one Spotted Face waited while the rest of the prisoners went on. Adoniram longed to be on a cart, too. His feet were a mass of bloody blisters, and the heat from the blazing sun made it nearly impossible for him to focus on his next step.

After two miles of walking, one of Henry's old servants came running up to see his master one last time. When he saw Adoniram's condition, he pulled the turban off his head and ripped it into pieces. The prisoners were not allowed to stop even for a moment, and so with great difficulty, the servant wrapped Adoniram's feet in cloth, and then he did the same for Henry Gouger. This eased the pain a little, and when the servant returned to help support Adoniram as he walked, the missionary sobbed quietly. During his time in prison he had become unused to such acts of human kindness.

Eventually, they reached Amarapura. The seven prisoners sat with their backs against a wall, glad to be stopped. They had walked only four miles, but because of their pitiful physical condition, it may as well have been four hundred miles. Soon a cart rumbled up with the Greek man on it. The man was dead.

Through a haze of pain and fever, Adoniram learned that they were to spend the night where they had stopped and go on to Oung-pen-la, a tiny village four miles away, the next day. However, by the following morning, none of the prisoners could move. The men were weak from hunger, and their feet and legs were swollen. By now the Spotted Faces had turned the prisoners over to the commander's guards and returned to the prison. The new guards soon realized that their prisoners could not be bullied into walking any farther. As a result, a cart was ordered to take them the rest of the way.

Even lying in the cart required tremendous effort. Every jolt jarred Adoniram's bony body until he was barely conscious. And even though they started out at daybreak, it was mid-afternoon, with the merciless sun baking down on them, before the cart squeaked to a halt outside a long, deserted hut. Like all Burmese huts, this one stood on stilts, and it took supreme effort for the seven prisoners to drag themselves up the steps and inside.

Inside, the roof had long since caved in, and the door had been torn off. Much to Adoniram's dismay, a bamboo pole ran down the center of the room. And a pile of leg irons sat in the corner. Once more they were in prison. Adoniram lay down quietly and allowed the leg irons to be clamped around his ankles. He felt so wretched, he didn't care; he was just relieved to be still. He began to lapse in and out of consciousness. At one point as he balanced on the edge of consciousness, he thought he saw Ann and three-month-old Maria standing over him. Ann was shaking him saying, "Wake up, Adoniram, wake up. I have come to see you."

Adoniram fought to keep himself from slipping further over the edge into unconsciousness. His eyes could barely focus, but his mind told him he was not dreaming—his faithful wife really had found him.

"Why have you come?" he mumbled in a daze. "I hoped you would not follow me here to see me die. You cannot stay." With that, Adoniram slipped into unconsciousness.

Adoniram remembered nothing more until after darkness had fallen. He awoke with his feet high above his head, hooked to the same kind of bamboo contraption that had been in the cell at the death prison. This time, though, the men had a new kind of torture to endure: mosquitoes. Their new prison was surrounded by rice paddies, and since it had no roof or door, the pests swarmed in to feast on the swollen and bloodied feet of the prisoners. The result was pure agony, especially since the prisoners' feet were too high off the ground for them to swat the hungry insects.

The night seemed to drag on forever, but eventually the sun rose. The prisoners were let down from the bamboo pole and invited to sit out on the veranda. Adoniram thought this was a good sign, although Henry Gouger was the only man with enough strength to crawl that far. Soon a group of men from the nearby village came to repair the collapsed roof, which was another encouraging sign for the prisoners. Perhaps they had not been brought here to be killed after all.

One of Dr. Price's friends arrived with a large bowl filled with cold rice and curry. The hungry prisoners gratefully devoured the food. Ann arrived later that morning, having spent the night in the village. This time Adoniram was fully conscious, glad to see her, and ready to ask questions.

Adoniram learned that Ann had come with two of the little Burmese girls she was looking after, as well as a helper, and, of course, baby Maria. Ann told Adoniram that she intended to stay close by so that she could give whatever aid possible to the men. She was still at the prison at lunchtime when Henry Gouger's baker arrived from Ava with biscuits and salted fish for the men to eat. As they ate together, Ann confided to Adoniram that it was the first food she had eaten in two days. Adoniram was appalled by the news. He looked at his wife and new daughter and wondered whether any of them would still be alive in a month.

[handwritten margin notes: "Ann is there?", "CC", "Why hadn't Ann eaten", "TQ"]

Chapter 17

The Black Seal

Rrrrrrroar! Adoniram turned his head slowly to the side and peered out between the slats on the wall. It sounded for all the world like a lion, he thought, but it couldn't be. He must be hearing things. He was not. In the distance he saw one of the strangest sights he'd ever seen in Burma. Four of his jailers were dragging a solid wheeled cart along a muddy track towards the prison hut. On the cart was a cage, and in the cage was a full-grown lion.

"Look at what's coming," Adoniram told Henry Gouger.

Henry wiggled himself around until he could see out the crack. "Oh," he groaned. "They're going to make quite a sport out of us, aren't they. No doubt

195

[handwritten margin notes: "!!", "A lion", "!!", "!!", "Henry thinks he's going to be fed to the lion"]

they will feed us to the lion when they have drawn a big enough crowd."

By now all seven men had resigned themselves to dying in custody, but the thought of being torn from limb to limb by a lion was still daunting for Adoniram. The prisoners waited all day, and the following day as well, to see what the purpose of the lion might be.

"The jailers won't go near it," observed Captain Laird.

"Maybe they captured it because the lion is the symbol of British power," suggested Adoniram. It would be a strange reason, but who knew what the Burmese officials were thinking these days?

The weeks went by, and lion's presence continued to be a mystery. No one fed the lion, and the hungrier the animal got, the more it roared. Sometimes it would roar all night long, and Adoniram would lie awake wondering whether the jailers were just getting it good and ready to eat them. But strangely, and much to everyone's relief, instead of the prisoners being fed to the hungry lion, the hungry lion died of starvation.

By now, the prisoners, who were being fed well by Henry Gouger's cook and watched over by Ann, were feeling a little stronger than they had in a long time. Their new jailers were not as vicious as the Spotted Faces and allowed them to go for short walks outside the prison hut (in chains, of course).

Soon after the lion died, Adoniram began to look closely at the cage it had been housed in. The cage was cool and clean, two things the prison hut

[Handwritten margin notes:]
setting
prepared to die, but not by a lion
!! ..
maybe they won't be fed to lions
TQ
won't be fed!
Fed well & watched over by Ann = stronger
Jailers not vicious
Lion cage = daunting cleaner than other prison hut

was not. Soon Adoniram got permission from the head jailer to move into the lion's cage, with the door locked securely behind him. He was even allowed to sleep there at night, which meant that for the first time in over a year he slept with his feet on the ground, not above his head.

It was the beginning of August before the men got any idea how the war with Great Britain was progressing. A group of officials descended on the prison and demanded that all the prisoners be taken immediately to Amarapura. Once there, the men were each housed in a separate cell. Adoniram wished he'd had time to say good-bye to Ann and Maria. He felt sure the end was near. Indeed, the end was near, though not the end of his life, as he thought, but the end of the war. King Bagyidaw had brought the foreign prisoners to Amarapura to translate papers outlining a treaty to end the war. The British had won, and Sir Archibald Campbell, commander of the British forces, had written out Britain's terms for Burma's surrender. However, the only people in the whole country who could translate these terms for the Burmese to understand them were the prisoners and Ann.

The surrender, which involved handing over several Burmese territories to Great Britain, took a long time to negotiate. It was November before the treaty was ratified and the foreign prisoners were finally set free.

The British, though, still had more translation work to do, so they asked Adoniram to visit their camp at Yandabo farther downriver to help out. A boat was provided for the trip, and soon the Judson family was floating serenely down the Irrawaddy River on a beautiful moonlit night. As Adoniram sat with his wife at his side and his baby daughter in his arms, he marveled at the sights and sounds around him. Every moment of life seemed extra precious to him now. He turned to Ann and with a sigh said, "Heaven must be something like this."

When they reached the British camp, Adoniram went straight to work translating the Treaty of Yandabo. His old friend, Henry Gouger, was already there helping with the translation, and the two of them worked side-by-side.

By March 1826, the work was done, and Adoniram and Ann were escorted back to Rangoon aboard the gunboat *Irrawaddy*. With all the fighting that had gone on around Rangoon, they wondered whether there would be anything remaining of the mission house they had left over two years before. When the British had bombarded the city, the Wades and the Houghs had been forced to flee to Calcutta, leaving the mission house unattended.

Amazingly, the house was still standing, though it was in bad shape. Adoniram stood in front of it, its doors torn off and many of its exterior boards broken, and wondered where he would find the strength to repair it. He also wondered where he would find the strength to begin work translating the New Testament into Burmese all over again.

Before the night was over, however, Adoniram was in for one of the most wonderful surprises of

[handwritten: took 9 yrs to translate NT]

his life. He learned that on the day the foreign prisoners were taken from the death prison, Maung Ing,
a faithful convert who had accompanied Adoniram
and Ann when they moved to Ava, had gone to
the prison to look for some token to remember
his American friend by. All he found was an old
pillow, too dirty and worn to be of use even to a
Spotted Face, and so the pillow had been thrown in
the mud outside the prison wall.

Maung Ing recognized it as Adoniram's pillow
and took it home to wash it. Only then did he notice
how unusually lumpy it felt. He investigated and
found the entire translation of the New Testament
into Burmese, which Adoniram had spent nine
years working to complete.

Overjoyed at the discovery, Maung Ing had kept
the manuscript safe. Now Adoniram was free, and
Ann was no longer under suspicion. It was time
to return the translation. Adoniram could hardly
believe the story, but there was no doubt it was true.
Maung Ing held the pages of the Burmese translation in his hands. Over the next few days, Adoniram
and Ann worked hard to locate the little band of
Christian converts they had left behind. Only Maung
Shway-gnong could be found. They had expected
this. The war had disrupted the lives of many people
in Burma, especially those in the coastal provinces.
As a result, people had been scattered to various
parts of the country. This led Adoniram and Ann to
ask an important question. Since the church had been
dispersed, should they stay in Rangoon to rebuild it,

[handwritten margin notes: Maung Ing; CC; !!; Ad. realizes his NT is w/ maung Ing; !!; !! can't find Ing; setting; TQ]

[handwritten at bottom: His NT is with Maung Ing !!!! TQ - should they stay and rebuild the church in Rangoon]

or should they move to Amherst? Now that things had settled down in Burma, the Wades had moved from Calcutta to Amherst.

Amherst was a brand-new city about one hundred miles southeast of Rangoon on the eastern shore of the Gulf of Martaban. It had been set up by the British to govern the parts of Burma they had won in the Treaty of Yandabo, and many Burmese people were moving there. Adoniram had been assured there would be no problems if he decided to establish a mission there. Indeed, Lord Amherst, the British governor general after whom the town was named, promised to give the missionaries his full support.

The offer was tempting. It meant there would be no more officials arriving at the door to collect some new tax, and no more "gifts" would have to be given to gain a hearing with a top government official. And there would be no worrying about their Burmese converts being harassed, since the British had promised religious freedom in Amherst.

On July 2, 1826, the Judson family arrived in Amherst, where they found board with an Englishman, Captain Fenwick. However, their time together there was short. The East India Company had plans for Adoniram—though not to deport him back to England, as they had tried to do in India years before, but to do translation work for them. They wanted Adoniram to aid them in translating and negotiating a trade arrangement with the Burmese government so that goods could be imported to and exported from the country. At first Adoniram flatly refused. His missionary work—not trade arrangements—was what mattered most to him. But now that Henry Gouger had left Burma, Adoniram was the only person in the country who could do the job. Finally, the East India Company made him an offer he couldn't refuse: not money, but the promise that along with the trade agreement the company would try to get the Burmese government to agree to religious freedom for every citizen in the country.

Even though it meant his returning to Ava and the family's being separated yet again, Adoniram and Ann agreed that it was a heaven-sent opportunity. Imagine, they told each other, if Burmese people were free to be Christians, there would be no more secret baptisms and no more whispered sermons behind closed doors. Adoniram waved to Ann from the deck of the small steamboat that was to take him upriver to Ava. He hoped the negotiations would go well so that he could be back with his family soon.

To Adoniram and Ann's dismay, the negotiations dragged on endlessly. The Burmese government haggled over every word in the agreement, and by October Adoniram was wondering whether he would ever get home to Ann and Maria. He eagerly awaited the arrival of each new letter from Ann. Some of the letters bothered him, however. Maria was sickly and weak, and sometimes Ann wrote about her concern that Maria would not live to see her second birthday.

[Handwritten margin notes: Henry = gone. made a deal w/ EIC. Religious freedom 4 all. Would have to return to Ava. People could be Christian freely. Left. A lot of translating had. Q would he return home? Maria = sick near death.

Bottom note: Religious freedom 4 all after Ad. agreed to translate for EIC (for trade, etc.) = move to Ava; Maria = sick]

November 24, 1826, was a day Adoniram would never forget. He was staying at Dr. Price's house in Ava when a servant handed him a letter. Adoniram's hand shook as he carried it to his room. The letter had a black seal, a customary way for the writer to let the reader know it brought news of a death. He thought of little Maria as he shut the door behind him, and he hoped that Ann had not become sick with grief. After all, Maria was their third child to die in infancy.

Reluctantly Adoniram broke the seal and opened the envelope to read the details. He noted that the letter was dated a month before, October 26, 1826. He read on: "My Dear Sir: To one who has suffered so much and with such exemplary fortitude, there needs but little preface to tell a tale of distress. It were cruel indeed to torture you with doubt and suspense. To sum up the unhappy tidings in a few words—*Mrs. Judson is no more.*"

Adoniram sat still, his eyes fixed on the words before him, trying desperately to grasp the meaning of what he had just read. *Mrs. Judson is no more.* Ann? The bride who had followed him to Burma? The woman who had risked everything to stay near him while he was in prison? His best friend in all the world? Ann was dead? It didn't seem possible.

After several motionless minutes, Adoniram read on. Ann had apparently developed a severe fever that the doctor could not cure. Despite the best medical care available, she had slipped into unconsciousness and died. Her body had been buried under a hopia tree. The letter went on to say that Maria was in the care of Jonathan and Deborah Wade, the missionary couple who had accompanied Ann back to Burma after her trip to New England three years before.

Adoniram folded the letter and laid his head on the desk. Tears flowed down his face and onto his jacket sleeve. He began to sob, quietly at first and then so loudly that Dr. Price came to see what the trouble was. There was nothing he could do to comfort Adoniram. Nothing could wipe away the words, *Mrs. Judson is no more.*

Only three days later, Dr. Price himself needed comfort when his Burmese wife, along with their baby, died during childbirth. Now the two men were widowers grieving together.

It was two months later, at the end of January 1827, before Adoniram's work for the East India Company was finished and he was free to return to Amherst. Adoniram felt bitter about his dealings with the East India Company. The final treaty had no clause guaranteeing religious freedom for all the people of Burma. Adoniram felt used and that his time had been wasted. This was not just any time that had been wasted; it had been his last opportunity to be with the only woman he had ever loved. The trip back downriver to Amherst was sad and lonely.

When Adoniram arrived and little Maria was brought out onto the veranda to be reunited with her father, she clung fearfully to Deborah Wade. It was obvious she did not recognize her own father. Adoniram wept, for he knew it would be only a matter of time before Maria forgot her mother as well.

Adoniram sought out Dr. Richardson, who had treated Ann until she died. In his opinion, the years of not eating enough or taking care of her health had weakened Ann to the point where a fever could kill her. This made Adoniram feel worse, not better. He was the one who had been in the death prison, yet ironically he had lived through the ordeal while the stress of the situation on Ann had helped to end her life.

Still, there was work to be done. The Baptist mission society in the United States was sending out more missionaries. Soon George Boardman and his beautiful blonde, blue-eyed wife, Sarah, arrived in Burma, along with their baby daughter.

More than ever, Adoniram felt the need to keep on with his translation work. As well, he preached several times a week in a hastily built zayat. Freed from the laws governing religion in the rest of Burma, many citizens of Amherst were eager to learn about the gospel. But despite all his busyness, Ann was never far from his thoughts.

Six months to the day after Ann's death, Maria died. She was two years, three months old. Adoniram buried her beside her mother. In July 1827, Adoniram received a letter from his mother informing him that his father had died. Although his father had been an old man, this was still a difficult death for Adoniram to cope with. Not

[handwritten margin notes: Maria doesn't know her mom or dad; Ad. lived thru prison, Ann stressed over Ad. = her death; More missionaries, new ppl; A&A; zayat; many eager to learn; 6 mo after Ann's death Maria dies; 1827 = Dad dead; new people — George & Sarah Boardman & baby; His (Ad.) church is growing again; Maria Dies]

long afterwards, he received word that his brother Elnathan, who was thirty-five years old, had died. Soon after that, Elnathan's widow and his only daughter also died. Such news greatly depressed Adoniram, who began to think that his mother would never have any grandchildren who lived past the age of ten. He also began to wonder about the point of living. Slowly he began to cut himself off from any social contact. He informed the governor and other British dignitaries that he no longer wanted to be invited to their parties.

By the second anniversary of Ann's death, Adoniram was spending his days sitting quietly in a jungle hut. The other missionaries tried to interest him in the daily running of the mission, but it was an uphill battle. All Adoniram wanted was to be left alone with his God and with the memories of his dead wife and children.

It was the beginning of 1830 before the cloud of depression began to lift from Adoniram. Cephas Bennett and his family arrived in Burma from the United States. Cephas was a printer, and once again Adoniram found his thoughts turning towards things the mission could print: tracts, the New Testament, and Psalms, which he had also translated. At the same time, he decided it was time to start focusing his attention back on translating the rest of the Old Testament.

About this time, word reached Adoniram that Dr. Price had died, leaving Sarah and George Boardman to care for his two children. By now the Boardmans were living in the highlands of Burma. They had two boys of their own, Judson and George, who had both been born in Burma. Their oldest child, Sarah, had died. It seemed to Adoniram that death was still all around him, but somehow he now had strength to go on with his missionary work. He decided to leave Amherst and its painful memories behind and move to Moulmein, about forty miles north of Amherst, where a small band of Burmese Christians needed a leader.

All around him, Adoniram saw encouraging signs that Burma was changing. In March, he traveled to Rangoon for the festival at Shwe Dagon pagoda. Cephas Bennett had printed ten thousand tracts for the occasion, and Adoniram distributed them all to people who asked. Six thousand people came to the mission house to ask questions about what they had read. Adoniram was delighted. He wrote of this in his journal:

> Some [inquirers] come two or three months' journey, from the borders of Siam and China—"Sir, we hear that there is an eternal hell. We are afraid of it. Do give us a writing that will tell us how to escape it." Others come from the frontiers of Kathay, a hundred miles north of Ava—"Sir, we have seen a writing that tells about an eternal God. Are you the man that gives away such writings? If so, pray give us one, for we want to know

the truth before we die." Others come from the interior of the country, where the name of Jesus Christ is little known— "Are you Jesus Christ's man? Give us a writing that tells about Jesus Christ."

Adoniram marveled at the change the war had made in the openness of the Burmese people to Christianity. It had taken him nine years of hard work to win the first eighteen Burmese converts. Now, in 1831 alone, there had been two hundred seventeen baptisms. This brought the total number of baptized Christians in Burma to two hundred forty Burmese and one hundred thirteen foreigners. Adoniram was only sorry that Ann was not at his side to see it all for herself.

[handwritten margin notes: "9 yrs = 18 Burmese converts", "religious freedom"]

[handwritten notes below text:]

Burmese Baptized Christians:
240
13 foreigners

Oct 26, 1826 = Ann = dead
Price's wife & kid = dead
July 1827 = Maria = dead
6 mo./1 later
Ad's dad = dead
Elnathan = dead
Elnathan's child = dead
Elnathan's widow = dead
Price = dead
Sarah (oldest of Boardman's children) dies

LHT (10) dead
LHT

Chapter 18

Sarah

More than anything, Adoniram liked to be out among the Burmese people handing out tracts, answering questions, and challenging Buddhist holy men. Yet he realized his most urgent work was that of Bible translation. While translation of the New Testament into Burmese was complete, he was only one third of the way through translating the Old Testament. So as much as he wanted to be out among the people, he set his sights on completing translation of the entire Bible. For the next two and a half years, Adoniram did his translation work six days a week. His goal was to translate thirty verses a day. This was a difficult task, because Adoniram did not take the easy route of translating from the English Bible into Burmese. Rather, he translated the

[handwritten margin notes: A&A, determined, smart, !!, translation, 1/3 OT, determined, A&A, wants to translate the whole Bible]

209

original Hebrew directly into Burmese. This made for a more accurate translation, but it took a lot more time and effort.

On January 31, 1834, the huge job was complete. In his hands Adoniram held a complete translation of the Bible in the Burmese language. Now he had to wait while it was typeset in Burmese type and printed. This was a painstaking task that could take anywhere from three to six years.

On completion of the translation, Adoniram received a letter of congratulation from Sarah Boardman. Soon after their arrival at Amherst, Sarah and her husband, George, had moved to the jungles of Burma. There they had worked among the Karen people, a native tribe who lived in large family groupings. Of all the people in Burma, the Karen were the most open to the gospel, and a number of them had been converted. Three years before, in 1831, George Boardman had died. The day before his death he baptized thirty-four Karen converts. Sarah Boardman decided to stay on alone in the jungle to carry on the missionary work her husband had begun among the Karen.

Now that Adoniram had more time on his hands, he began corresponding with Sarah Boardman. Their letters quickly became more personal, until in March Adoniram wrote asking Sarah to marry him. She agreed, and the two of them were married on April 1, 1834. Adoniram was forty-five years old, and Sarah was thirty. Neither of them knew whether they would spend a few months or many years together, but they were both glad to have found someone to share their lives with.

In December that year, Sarah sent her only surviving child, George, back to the United States. Her other son, Judson, had died several years before in the jungle, as had Dr. Price's two children, whom the Boardmans had been raising. Sarah had been planning to send George home for some time because she thought the healthier climate there was the best chance her son had at reaching adulthood. Both she and Adoniram were sad to see seven-year-old George leave. They didn't know when they would see him again. As it turned out, one of them would see him again, and one would not.

Adoniram and Sarah moved into a three-room house in Moulmein. Like Ann, Sarah had a flare for languages. She set about learning Taling, a tribal language spoken in Burma, in the hopes that one day gospel literature could be translated into this language, too. Adoniram was also busy. The local church now had one hundred members, and during the week, classes were held in everything from prayer to learning English.

On October 31, 1835, another Judson baby was born. Adoniram named her Abigail Ann, after his mother and his first wife. Three more children followed in quick succession: Adoniram Jr. on April 7, 1837, Elnathan on July 15, 1838, and Henry on December 31, 1839.

In October 1840, Adoniram finally had in his hands a bound copy of the Burmese Bible, all twelve hundred pages of it. It was now twenty-seven years since he and Ann had stepped off the *Georgiana* in Rangoon and first heard the Burmese language spoken. Adoniram had struggled to learn the language at first, but the struggle had been worth it. Now the Burmese could read about God and Jesus and salvation in their own language. It was Adoniram's greatest achievement with the Burmese language.

In 1840, Sarah was expecting another baby, though this time it ended in sadness. They named the stillborn child Luther. Soon afterwards, Sarah became ill with dysentery, as did all of the children. Since nothing could be done for the disease in Burma, the doctor recommended they take a trip to Serampore, where a slight change in climate might help.

The journey to Calcutta was perilous, and included the ship's being caught on a sandbar. Eventually, though, the family made it to Serampore alive, and once there, Sarah's health began to improve. The children's health began to improve, too, all except one-year-old Henry. The boy continued to get sicker and weaker, until on July 31, 1841, he died quietly in his sleep. Adoniram and Sarah buried their young son in the mission cemetery at Serampore alongside the graves of William Carey, William Ward, and Joshua Marshman, the three men who had so greatly helped and influenced Adoniram and Ann when they had arrived in Calcutta twenty-nine years before on their way to be missionaries in Burma. With great sadness the Judson family returned to Burma.

In July the following year, another son was born to Adoniram and Sarah. They named him Henry in honor of the brother he would never know. Adoniram and Sarah had two more sons, Charles, born December 18, 1843, and Edward, born December 27, 1844. This meant that Adoniram now had six living children, and Sarah, seven. However, counting the children who had died, Sarah had actually given birth to eleven children, and those births, along with the harsh conditions of Burma, had taken a toll on her body. She caught every illness that circulated in Moulmein, and long bouts of dysentery often kept her in bed for weeks at a time.

By March 1845, both Adoniram's and Sarah's health were in a weakened state. The ongoing bouts of sickness were causing Sarah to fade fast. Adoniram had a throat and chest infection that caused him to cough continually, and he could not speak above a whisper. The doctor warned Sarah that her only hope for recovery was to get back to the United States for treatment as quickly as possible. By April she was too sick to travel alone, so Adoniram made plans to return to America with Sarah and the three oldest children, Abigail, Adoniram Jr., and Elnathan. The three youngest children, Henry, Charles, and four-month-old Edward would stay behind with various missionary families.

On April 26, 1845, five members of the Judson family climbed aboard the *Paragon*. If all went well, when Adoniram and Sarah returned to Burma, the three oldest children would stay on in the United States. So it was with great sadness that they said farewell to the three youngest children. Adoniram realized it was probably the last time he would ever see his entire family together in one place. The only bright spot about the impending voyage was the knowledge that Sarah's son George would be waiting for them in Boston. George was now eighteen years old, and as sad as she was to leave her three littlest children behind, Sarah was excited about seeing her oldest son again.

The voyage seemed to work wonders on Adoniram's and the children's health. Three weeks after setting sail, the children were playing tag on the foredeck and enjoying themselves immensely. Things were not going so well for Sarah, though. Sometimes she appeared to be improving, and then she would get sicker than she had been before.

By the time the ship dropped anchor in St. James Bay on the island of St. Helena in the south Atlantic, Adoniram was convinced Sarah was near death. Indeed she was, and in the early hours of September 1, 1845, Sarah Judson died. A coffin was rowed out to the ship and Sarah's body placed in it. Adoniram, the three oldest Judson children, and many members of the crew escorted the body ashore. A local missionary conducted a funeral service, and Sarah was buried in the church cemetery. That night, Adoniram, his heart breaking, and the children returned to the ship, which immediately set sail for Boston.

The end had come so quickly for Sarah that Adoniram and the children could scarcely believe she was really dead and buried and that they were continuing on without her. A week later Adoniram wrote in his journal: "For a few days, in the solitude of my cabin, with my poor children crying around me, I could not help abandoning myself to heart-breaking sorrow. But the promise of the Gospel came to my aid, and faith stretched her view to the bright world of eternal life..."

Once again, Adoniram Judson, now fifty-seven years old, was a widower. This time, however, he had been left with the responsibility of six children of his own and one of Sarah's. He wondered what he would do with the children when he reached Boston. His mother had died several years before, but his sister Abigail was still alive. She was now fifty-four years old, and Adoniram wondered whether she would be up to caring for his three lively children.

None of the children spoke much English, since Adoniram and Sarah had always spoken Burmese around the home. Adoniram was even a little worried about carrying on a long conversation in English and fitting in with American ways. After all, it had been thirty-three years since he had last set foot in his homeland. It seemed to him, too, that almost everyone he had known in New England was now dead. The "three Samuels"—Samuel Nott, Samuel Mills, and Samuel Newell, who in 1810 had signed their names along with his to the petition to the General Assembly of the Congregational Church requesting that they form a missionary society—were now faded memories. Samuel Mills had died at sea in 1818 while returning to Africa where he had been a missionary. Samuel Newell had died in India soon after leaving Adoniram and Ann and Luther Rice on the Isle of France. And as far as Adoniram was aware, Samuel Nott had died in India, too.

It was a Wednesday afternoon in mid-October when Adoniram and his three children finally stepped ashore in Boston. Thousands of people lined the dock and spilled out into the street beyond. Many of them carried a copy of Ann Judson's biography, which had been reprinted many times and circulated throughout the United States.

Adoniram gulped, and tears welled in his eyes as he looked out at the cheering crowd. He realized that far from being a forgotten figure in history, he, along with the other early American foreign missionaries, had become a hero. It was gratifying to know people thought of him that way, though he did not consider himself a hero. He had simply done what he believed God had called him to do.

As Adoniram helped the children ashore in their new homeland, the crowd hushed, waiting for the veteran missionary to address them. Adoniram cleared his throat and opened his mouth to speak, but nothing more than a whisper came out. A pastor standing close by stepped forward and yelled Adoniram's words of greeting, gratitude, and thanks to the crowd. When he was done, the crowd once again cheered wildly.

That night, as Adoniram lay alone in bed, his thoughts drifted back to the time he and Ann had stood together on the deck of the *Caravan* and watched the coast of New England fade from view. The newly married couple was barely out of their teens at the time and were filled with enthusiasm to spread the gospel. Now Ann was gone, along with the three children she had given birth to. And now Sarah was dead, too, along with three more of Adoniram's children. Adoniram had paid a higher price than he could ever have imagined, yet the rewards were great. He had left behind him in Burma a complete translation of the Bible in the Burmese language, a strong contingent of missionaries, and hundreds of converts. Now he wondered what lay ahead of him. Would he see his adopted country and his three youngest children again?

The following few days in Boston were hectic. It seemed that everyone wanted to see the "Saint of Burma," as Adoniram had been dubbed by the press. Adoniram was horrified by the title. He knew he had made many mistakes along the way, and he worried that people would think he was perfect. Adoniram attended meetings every day, sometimes going to as many as three or four. After a while the meetings all seemed to blur together in his mind, though one meeting would forever stand out in his memory. He had just finished speaking when an elderly man rose from the congregation and made his way to the front of the church. Adoniram stared; there was something vaguely familiar about the man. Suddenly, as the man climbed onto the platform, Adoniram realized who he was. It was Samuel Nott! The two men embraced. Many in the congregation wiped away tears as they watched the reunion of these two great Christian men.

Later Samuel Nott explained to Adoniram that reports of his death in India had been premature. He had become gravely ill there and eventually returned to the United States, where he had made a full recovery. Since then he had served as a Congregational pastor in Wareham, Massachusetts.

A week after arriving in Boston, Adoniram and the children were glad to board a train for Bradford to visit Ann's mother and sisters, Mary and Abigail. Of course, there was the inevitable round of meetings in Bradford, and soon Adoniram began to feel like a caged zoo animal on display. He longed for some peace and quiet, as did his children. The children were often left with strangers while he was away at speaking engagements, and they were finding it difficult to adjust to life in New England. Adoniram decided the sooner he could get them settled, the better off they would be.

After much consideration he decided to send the boys to live with Dr. and Mrs. Newton, friends of Sarah's. George Boardman, the boys' half brother, was already staying there, and the Newtons were happy to accept the responsibility of two more children. Adoniram had already decided that Abigail Ann, who was just about to celebrate her tenth birthday, should stay with his sister Abigail in Plymouth.

When he arrived in Plymouth to deliver his daughter, Adoniram was surprised by what he found. Abigail still lived in his parents' house, and the room he had grown up in with Elnathan was still there, exactly as he had left it thirty-three years before. Abigail had refused to let anyone touch a thing. Walking into his boyhood bedroom gave Adoniram the eerie feeling of moving back in time.

A letter was waiting for Adoniram in Plymouth. It was from Burma, and it was not good news. Charles, the middle of the three youngest Judson children, had died soon after the rest of the family set sail for the United States. Charles had actually died a month before Sarah, and Adoniram breathed a prayer of thanks that Sarah never knew about it and never had to bear the grief of her son's death as she herself lay ill.

By midwinter, Adoniram's thoughts were turning back towards Burma and the two children he had not seen in nine months. The three older children were now settled into their new homes, and there was little more he could do for them. But before he could set sail again for Burma, there were still more meetings for him to speak at. In one particular case, a Reverend Mr. Gillette from the Eleventh Street Baptist Church in Philadelphia had written several times asking Adoniram to come and speak. Adoniram's voice had still not returned to normal, and he wondered wearily why so many people still wanted to hear him speak. He kept putting off making a decision about going to speak in

Philadelphia, but the Reverend Mr. Gillette was a persistent man. When he wrote again and said he would take the train to Plymouth and personally escort Adoniram back to Philadelphia, Adoniram felt it would be impolite to refuse his offer.

The train ride from Plymouth to New York went as planned, but the trip from New York to Philadelphia took two hours longer than normal because of a derailment ahead. They were two hours that would change the course of Adoniram's life.

Chapter 19

Homeward Bound

LI

The train hissed to a stop, and Adoniram glanced at the Reverend Mr. Gillette, who looked apologetic. "I don't know what the holdup is. Let's hope it won't be long," he said.

train late— stopped

Adoniram nodded just as the conductor entered their carriage.

"Derailment on the line ahead. They're clearing it now. Should be done in an hour or two," announced the conductor with a strong Irish accent as he walked briskly down the aisle on his way to the next carriage.

LI Derailment

"It looks like we'll be sitting here awhile," said Mr. Gillette. "I wish I'd brought some work with me."

"Me too," lamented Adoniram. "For once in my life I don't have a single thing to read."

A$A oh, smart Adi

Mr. Gillette pulled his leather satchel from the rack above his head and reached inside. "I'm sure this isn't along your usual tastes, Dr. Judson, but you are welcome to take a look at it if you would like."

Adoniram took the slim, leather-bound book the pastor was holding out to him. "*Tripping in Author Land*," he read aloud, "by Fanny Forester. You're right. It's not my usual fare, but thank you for the thought."

He opened the book and skimmed through the chapter titles, *The Bank Note*, *Nickie Ben*, and *The Chief's Daughter*. Nothing Adoniram would want to read caught his eye, but since there was little else to do, he flipped to the middle of the book and began to read. Soon he was totally engrossed. The stories themselves were flimsy tales, something his daughter Abigail might read, he thought, but there was something about the writing style itself. The book was filled with humor and lightness, and Adoniram found himself feeling sorry that the author had wasted her talents on such trivial material.

After he had read for a while, Adoniram looked up. "Very good writing," he said to his traveling companion. "Fanny Forester certainly has a way with words. Do you know if she is a Christian?"

"Yes," replied the pastor, "I know for a fact she is. Her real name is Emily Chubbock, and she used to be a teacher in a seminary before she took to writing."

"What a pity," sighed Adoniram, and then a plan began to form in his mind. "I wish I could meet her."

Mr. Gillette laughed loudly. "That can most certainly be arranged," he exclaimed. "She is staying at my house right now!"

Adoniram chuckled. "Well, how is that for providence?" he said.

The following day, Christmas Day 1845, Adoniram got to meet Emily Chubbock. Emily was about thirty years old, with long black hair. Adoniram noted she was not particularly pretty, yet her sense of humor shone through in her personality, just as it had in her books. Adoniram was surprised to learn she had been a Baptist all her life and had made it a point to read all the newsletters published by the Baptist mission society that told the story of his life in Burma.

This was what Adoniram had been waiting to hear. Since arriving back in the United States he had been praying he would meet the right person to write a biography of his late wife Sarah. Now, looking at Emily Chubbock, he felt sure that God had answered his prayers.

Adoniram stayed on in Philadelphia to help Emily make an outline of Sarah's life and to answer the many questions she had about life in Burma. It seemed the more time Emily spent with Adoniram, the more she grew to respect and then love him. As strange as the match may have seemed to others, thirty-year-old romance writer Emily Chubbock, alias Fanny Forester, and Adoniram Judson, a fifty-seven-year-old missionary, had fallen in love. Emily agreed to marry Adoniram and return with him to Burma and help raise his two small sons.

When word of the impending marriage reached the newspapers, it sent people all over the United States into an uproar. "How could a frothy writer like Fanny Forester possibly fit in as a missionary's wife?" people asked. Others wanted to know whether it was a fitting match for someone with Adoniram's public standing. After all, he was old enough to be her father! Emily Chubbock's readers were upset, too. Why was such an aspiring writer going to throw her life away to live in some far-off country? They thought she should stay in America and keep writing. Adoniram didn't care one bit what people thought or said. Emily Chubbock had agreed to marry him, and that was all that mattered.

The wedding took place June 2, 1846. The newlyweds spent a few quiet days together before visiting New York, Boston, Plymouth, and Bradford for a round of final farewells.

As the *Faneuil Hall* weighed anchor in Boston Harbor, Adoniram and Emily, the new Dr. and Mrs. Judson, waved from the ship's railing to the hundreds of people who had gathered to see them off. Adoniram felt sure it would be the last time he ever saw his native homeland, and he stood on deck long after the scene had faded from view. As he stood there, he thought about the last time he had watched America recede from view. The other three people who had stood with him on the deck of that ship were all dead. Now a new wife stood at his side. She had not even been alive when he and Ann had first ventured out for Burma.

The voyage "home" was a happy one. Emily was curious about everything aboard ship, and she did not suffer from seasickness at all. When they finally arrived back in Moulmein, they found Adoniram's two boys, Henry and Edward, healthy and well taken care of. The boys took to Emily right away, the memory of their own mother having faded to a distant shadow.

Soon after arriving back in Burma, Adoniram decided to move his family to Rangoon. He had begun work on a more complete Burmese-to-English dictionary, and there were many Burmese language scholars in Rangoon who could help him with the exact meaning of certain words.

Emily was happy to move, and she kept a meticulous and colorful diary of all that went on. When she finally arrived at the house in Rangoon she wrote: "We are blessed with our full share of cockroaches, beetles, lizards, rats, mosquitoes, and bedbugs. With the last the woodwork is alive...perhaps twenty have crossed my paper since I have been writing."

Emily also went on to describe the ongoing battle with bats in the rafters: "We have had men at work nearly a week trying to thin [the bats] out, and have killed a great many hundreds.... Everything, walls, tables, chairs, etc., are stained by them."

Still, Emily was determined not to complain or to compare her new life with her old one in America. She worked hard at raising the children. She also worked hard at writing the biography of

Sarah, grateful as she did so to be living in the land she was writing about.

On the first anniversary of their marriage, Emily wrote home to her sister: "It has been far the happiest year of my life; and, what is in my eyes still more important, my husband says it has been among the happiest of his."

As Adoniram continued to work on the dictionary, he tried to locate the Burmese Christians he had left behind years before. This proved difficult. A new governor was now ruling over Rangoon. He and his underlings had a wide range of torture techniques at their disposal which they seemed eager to use on anyone in the city and surrounding area who was seen to be "favoring Jesus Christ's religion." The small band of about twenty Christians left in Rangoon dared not meet together, or even know each other's names. Adoniram met with them separately or occasionally in groups of two or three at a time.

Living expenses in Rangoon were high, and the family found themselves dining mostly on rice and fruit and occasionally an unknown meat, which was later identified as rat meat.

When the rainy season arrived, Emily became ill. Each day it took almost every ounce of energy she had to write a page of Sarah's biography. She would have to take long rests between sentences. However, Adoniram suffered much more. One Saturday night his stomach began cramping in excruciating pain. Although he had seen many sick missionaries in the past, neither he nor Emily could work out what was wrong with him. They tried all the usual treatments, laudanum shots, rhubarb, and calomel, but nothing stopped the searing pain.

Eventually the illness left him, though he was weak for a long time. As he lay recovering, Adoniram thought about all the obstacles he had faced in Burma. Now, as he had when he translated the Old Testament into Burmese, he felt he needed to concentrate whatever energy he had left on revising the Burmese-to-English dictionary. Other missionaries would follow to Rangoon, and a thorough, well-written Burmese dictionary would make their job a lot easier.

On August 31, 1847, the Judson family packed up and returned to Moulmein. Moulmein was much smaller than Rangoon and provided a much easier environment in which to live. Emily was relieved to be moving. She was expecting a baby soon and would be glad to be living closer to Amherst and its European doctor.

Baby Emily Frances Judson was born the day before Christmas, 1847. She was a healthy child who thrived from the beginning. Adoniram and Emily were both very proud of her.

By now Emily had finished the biography of Sarah, and the manuscript had been sent to the United States for publication.

The family struggled on in Moulmein. Sometimes Adoniram would be ill for weeks on end, and other times Emily would be laid low by some sickness.

[handwritten marginal notes: no cure?; mm; Returned to moulmein; Expecting a baby; bio of Sarah = done; ill]

[handwritten at bottom: Emily Frances Judson born Dec. 24, 1847]

Whenever they were well enough, they went about their duties—Adoniram to work on his dictionary and Emily to looking after the children and learning the Burmese language.

By March 1850, Dr. Morton, the family's physician, was very worried about Adoniram's health. Adoniram was weak and vomited often. The doctor suggested a sea voyage as the only hope of cure. Since Emily, who was expecting their second child any day, was unable to go with him, Thomas Ranney, who oversaw the printing press for the mission, offered to accompany Adoniram on the voyage.

Adoniram's symptoms became worse; his feet swelled, and then the entire left side of his body. Emily began to suspect he was dying, and so the night before he was due to set sail, she asked him if he was prepared for the possibility of death.

Adoniram replied, "I am not tired of my work; neither am I tired of the world. Yet when Christ calls me home, I shall go with the gladness of a boy bounding away from his school!"

On Wednesday, April 3, 1850, sixty-one-year-old Adoniram was carried aboard the French barque Astride Marie, bound for the Isle of France. It was a sobering moment. The church members gathered at the dock to beg him not to go. They told him they could not bear the thought of his being buried at sea with no grave for them to visit. Adoniram sympathized with them, but the doctor had told him that a voyage was his only hope for survival, and he felt it would be wrong not to do all he could to live.

Nine days out to sea, on April 12, 1850, Adoniram Judson died. The ship's carpenter made a rough coffin, and Adoniram's body was placed inside the coffin, which was slid overboard that same evening. There were no hymns, no prayers, no speeches, no dramatic good-byes, just a few simple words muttered by the French captain of the *Astride Marie* as the ship sailed by the Andaman Islands. Ironically, Adoniram was buried at sea in almost the same spot that his and Ann's first child had been buried on their first voyage to Burma thirty-seven years before.

Ten days later, back in Moulmein, Emily Judson gave birth to a second child, a son whom she named Charles but who died that same day. Four months later, at the end of August, she received word that Adoniram had died. After giving it much thought, Emily decided to take the three children (two of Adoniram and Sarah's and her own daughter Emily) back to the United States. They arrived home in October, 1851.

Emily immediately set about helping the president of Brown University with the biography he was writing of her late husband. After her time in Burma, however, she was never healthy again, and soon after her arrival home she was diagnosed with tuberculosis. Two and a half years later, on June 1, 1854, Emily Judson, also known as Fanny Forester, died.

The three children Emily brought home with her from Burma all lived into adulthood. Henry fought for the Union Army in the Civil War, during which he was seriously injured. Edward became a pastor, and Emily's only child, Emily Frances, became a wife and mother. The three children Adoniram had left in America on his trip home also thrived. Like her aunt before her, Abigail became headmistress of Bradford Academy. Adoniram Jr. became a doctor, and Elnathan became a pastor. George Boardman Jr., Sarah and George Boardman's son, also became a pastor.

The translation of the Bible that Adoniram Judson worked so hard to complete remains to this day the only translation of the Bible into Burmese.

Henry = fought for Union in Civil War
Edward = pastor
Emily Frances = wife & mother
Abigail = headmistress of Brown University
Ad. Jr. = doctor
Elnathan = pastor
George Boardman Jr = pastor

Wow!

Bibliography

Anderson, Courtney. *To the Golden Shore*. Little, Brown and Company, 1956.

Hubbard, Ethel Daniels. *Ann of Ava*. Friendship Press, 1941.

Knowles, James D. *Memoir of Mrs. Ann H. Judson*. Lincoln & Edmands, 1831.

Stocker, Fern Neal. *Adoniram Judson: Following God's Plan*. Moody Press, 1986.

About the Authors

Janet and Geoff Benge are a husband and wife writing team with more than thirty years of writing experience. Janet is a former elementary school teacher. Geoff holds a degree in history. Originally from New Zealand, the Benges spent ten years serving with Youth With A Mission. They have two daughters, Laura and Shannon, and an adopted son, Lito. They make their home in the Orlando, Florida, area.

Also from Janet and Geoff Benge...

More adventure-filled biographies for ages 10 to 100!

Isobel Kuhn: On the Roof of the World • 978-1-57658-497-2
Elisabeth Elliot: Joyful Surrender • 978-1-57658-513-9
Paul Brand: Helping Hands • 978-1-57658-536-8
D. L. Moody: Bringing Souls to Christ • 978-1-57658-552-8
Dietrich Bonhoeffer: In the Midst of Wickedness • 978-1-57658-713-3
Klaus-Dieter John: Hope in the Land of the Incas • 978-1-57658-826-2

Available in paperback, e-book, and audiobook formats.
Unit Study Curriculum Guides are available for select biographies.
www.ywampublishing.com